Showing
America a New
Way Home

James A. Johnson

Foreword by Representative
James A. Leach, Chairman,
House Committee on Banking
and Financial Services

Showing America a New Way Home

Expanding Opportunities for Home Ownership

Jossey-Bass Publishers
San Francisco

Substantial discounts on bulk quantities of Jossey-Bass books are available to corporations, professional associations, and other organizations. For details and discount information, contact the special sales department at Jossey-Bass Inc., Publishers (415) 433–1740; Fax (800) 605–2665.

For sales outside the United States, please contact your local Simon & Schuster International Office.

 Manufactured in the United States of America on Lyons Falls Pathfinder Tradebook. This paper is acid-free and 100 percent totally chlorine-free.

Library of Congress Cataloging-in-Publication Data

Johnson, James A., date.
    Showing America a new way home : expanding opportunities for home ownership / James A. Johnson. — 1st ed.
       p.   cm. — (Jossey-Bass public administration series)
    Includes bibliographical references and index.
    ISBN 0–7879–0272–1
    1. Home ownership—United States.   2. Housing—United States—Finance.   3. Housing policy—United States.   4. Federal National Mortgage Association.   I. Title.   II. Series.
HD7287.82.U6J64   1996
363.5'83—dc20
                                      96–14977

HB Printing 10 9 8 7 6 5 4 3 2 1   FIRST EDITION

Contents

Foreword

O nce in a great while a book comes along that helps us look at a familiar institution with fresh eyes. *Showing America a New Way Home: Expanding Opportunities for Home Ownership* is just such a book. In it, Jim Johnson makes a compelling case for providing millions more American families with the opportunity to join that most American of institutions—family home ownership.

The American dream of owning one's home is deeply ingrained in the fabric of our national life. From colonial times through the present day, Americans have uniquely viewed the home less as shelter than as the encapsulation of the basic values of freedom and family.

John Locke, the philosophical godfather of Thomas Jefferson, asserted that the commonsense rights of seventeenth-century Englishmen related to life, liberty, and property. Jefferson, the dreamer, framed the American tradition with a profoundly revolutionary modification of Lockean verbiage: the notion that individuals are endowed by a Creator with inalienable rights, among them life, liberty, and the pursuit of happiness. The implicit connection of "property" with "pursuit of happiness," as well as the emphasis placed on the precept that the rights of the individual precede those of the state, led to the assumption that in America a person's home is a castle, the sanctity of which the state treads upon at great risk.

Home is about freedom. It is also about opportunity. Whereas our first century was all about establishing a society based on the rights of the individual, and our second century about assuring that such rights applied to peoples of all skin colors and both sexes, our third century is about opportunity, the insistence that rights, to be meaningful, must include everybody getting a fair crack at the American dream.

This book reflects the values the author grew up with as a small-town Midwestern Lutheran. It reflects the experience of an individual who, by dint of ability and commitment, has come to head the world's greatest institutional engine for home ownership—Fannie Mae. Its value lies in the clarity with which it both points out the tools now available for achieving home ownership and the reasonableness of the proposals advanced for putting this goal within the reach of more of our citizens. Thus this book lights a lamp of hope.

It is a moral imperative for society to ensure that groups of Americans are not left without realistic means of participating in this central facet of the American dream. Ways exist today to advance home ownership aspirations everywhere: from the inner cities to the suburbs, from the Sun Belt to Alaska; at issue is the commitment to developing the programmatic flexibility to meet changing economic circumstances. Some of the new housing initiatives suggested may generate controversy, but what is impressive is how practical those advanced in this book are and how significant the end result of their implementation is likely to be.

To buy a home is to "set down roots." It is an act of hope—one that reveals a deep faith in one's self, one's neighbors, and one's country. Home ownership should be part of, not beyond the means of, the life of every American family.

June 1996   —Representative James A. Leach
                               Chairman, House Committee on
                               Banking and Financial Services

Acknowledgments

I want to express my profound respect and admiration for the men and women at Fannie Mae who share my commitment to the American dream of home ownership and are working so hard to make it a reality for more American families than ever before. The home ownership strategy outlined in this book has its roots in their vast experience, wisdom, and creativity.

This book could not have been written without the help of several very talented individuals. Mary Cannon worked closely with me every step of the way; her assistance was invaluable. We were fortunate to have the help of a very bright and energetic researcher, Stuart Anderson. John Buckley was a trusted adviser throughout the process, and Bob Shrum, a friend for more than twenty-five years, shared his insights and his considerable editing skills with us at a critical point in the process. My friend Richard Leone was instrumental in getting the manuscript considered by Jossey-Bass. I owe a deep debt of gratitude to them all.

I also am indebted to my friend and colleague, David Maxwell, who launched Fannie Mae's special commitment to affordable housing in 1987. It was David Maxwell who initiated and guided the board decisions that led to my succeeding him as chairman and CEO of Fannie Mae; without him, I would not have been in the position to write this book.

I want to recognize the contributions of the many men and women in Congress, the administration, and throughout the housing industry who truly have been collaborators and partners in developing the ideas this book is based on. Special thanks go to the two men who have served as secretary of housing and urban development during my tenure as chairman and CEO—Henry Cisneros and Jack Kemp. Although they are members of different parties, both have recognized the importance of home ownership to the future of our nation and have worked passionately to extend its benefits to the American people.

Finally, I want to thank Cherry Billings, who has been my trusted personal assistant for fifteen years; Alan Shrader and the editorial staff at Jossey-Bass; and John DiQuollo, Lawrence Q. Newton, and Sylvia O'Brien of Fannie Mae for all their help in preparing this book for publication.

—J.A.J.

Showing
America a New
Way Home

To Maxine and Alfred, with all my love

Introduction

A home is perhaps the most personal of all our possessions. It is also a defining aspiration for almost all Americans. It's an investment, the biggest one most people will ever make. It's a place on the land—but also a place in the heart.

As chairman of Fannie Mae, the federally chartered, privately owned company that finances one of every five new mortgages generated in the nation each year, I'm in the business of helping people own their own home. I'll write about Fannie Mae at several points in this book, but that isn't my principal purpose. Instead, I want to look at U.S. home ownership as a whole—its history, its meaning, its current extent, and its possibilities for the future.

Most Americans probably don't realize the extent to which home ownership—the reality and the hope—is a hallmark of American society. Sixty-five percent of American families own their own home.[1] Yet for all that this fact implies, and for all that's been written about the subject (usually in technical journals), there's been little written and less read about the subject at a general-interest level. Americans live in, invest in, prize, and protect their homes, but they don't read much more about home ownership than what's in their own mortgage papers.

I hope that this book will offer a chance to change that. I also hope to outline an effective strategy that will broaden access to home ownership for millions of additional Americans who don't now own a home but could if the government and private institutions alike were to act with resolve, adaptability, and sensitivity. I begin by examining American attitudes toward home ownership and reviewing its history in the United States—how home ownership relates to the culture, economics, and political landscape of the nation. What expectations, hopes, and worries do Americans of the 1990s have about home ownership? What is their image of it? How is all this changing, and how is it changing the nation? In a very real sense, home ownership is implicitly rooted in America's founding ideals. John Locke, who inspired the nation's founders, wrote of the inalienable rights of "life, liberty, and property."[2] In the Declaration of Independence, Thomas Jefferson changed the last of these to "the pursuit of happiness." But he was encompassing and expanding—not supplanting—Locke's original notion, and property rights were later guaranteed in the Bill of Rights. In those first years, most Americans' property consisted almost entirely of their land, their farms, their houses—their "real estate," which is where the term came from in the first place.

Of course, the ideal was not always realized. It was insecure title protection in Kentucky that cost Abraham Lincoln's father the family home. Young Abe moved on to Indiana and then to Illinois, where he started a political career that brought him to the White House. The threat to capitalism engendered by the Great Depression was resolved not by abandoning the ideal of private property but by strengthening and broadening it, resulting in the greatest ownership of property—primarily homes—in any society in human history.

Indeed, American history is also the history of the greatest home ownership revolution ever known: this is a nation of home owners, actual or aspiring—and to the extent that this distinctive national characteristic is threatened, so is the prosperity and ultimately the stability of our society.

I grew up believing that home ownership was as American as the flag and the Fourth of July. My paternal grandparents came to

Swift County, Minnesota, from Norway in the 1870s. The log cabin my grandmother lived in on the prairie south of the small town of Benson has been preserved and restored by the Swift County Historical Society. With her parents and her five brothers and sisters, she lived in this one-room, unheated cabin on the prairie. Stand inside in the winter, and you'll know that the prairie wind is nearly unbearable.

The cabin was "discovered" about twenty-five years ago when the owners of an old farmhouse began knocking it down by hand. They had no wrecking crane. When they got to the kitchen, they used crowbars to peel off the wallboard, trying to knock holes here and there to get some leverage to tear the room apart. They couldn't get anywhere. It turned out that their kitchen had been built around the original log cabin—its inside and outside walls surrounded the logs. Nobody knew the log cabin was still there.

Once the wreckers realized what was there, the house was carefully disassembled around it. The cabin, which is now in the county's historical museum, conveys a real sense of heritage for the extended Johnson family and everyone in the area. My father spent his entire life, seventy-nine years, in Benson. His brothers and sisters lived their entire lives in Benson. Now when I take my son, Alfred, back home to Minnesota, we sometimes visit the museum. He's amazed to think, "This is where my great-grandmother lived and grew up."

The homes have changed, but the ideal of home ownership remains—from urban neighborhoods to the suburbs to small Midwestern towns, where the log cabins have long since given way to lumber and brick.

Too often, however, financial means and personal character count for far less in finding or buying a home than do prejudice and skin color. There are laws on credit and housing discrimination, and our nation needs to enforce them. There is prejudice in the real estate and mortgage markets, but there are also ways to counter it. We must pursue powerful policies that will increase the rate of home ownership among minorities to equal that of whites. I believe noth-ing would do more to advance social justice, heal the wounds of past discrimination, and bank the fires of future tension and division than to ensure truly equal access to home ownership.

We must increase home ownership not only for minorities but also among all Americans. Above all, this book proposes a strategy for increased home ownership. It argues the importance of home ownership as a key to individual work and community values. It relates home ownership to civic participation, better education, eco-nomic opportunity, and savings and investment. Home ownership, the reality and the aspiration, is itself an important family value—in many ways it is the bedrock of all the others.

The notion of a home ownership strategy raises an important question: what should be the nation's home ownership goal? The answer depends in part on how many Americans really want to own their own home. At Fannie Mae, we enlisted two of the nation's top pollsters, Democrat Peter Hart and Republican Bob Teeter, to answer that question.

They asked current renters whether they rent more as a matter of choice (that is, they could buy a home but choose to rent in-stead) or more as a result of circumstances (that is, they cannot afford to own a home right now). As it turns out, renting is largely a necessity, not a choice. Over 67 percent of renters said they would choose to own their home, and they rent only because they have to. If we add this group of would-be home owners to those who already own, we achieve a potential home ownership rate of 88 per-cent.[3] Perhaps no other aspiration in American life is so widely shared across all regions, classes, and age groups.

To achieve 88 percent home ownership would require a sudden leap in ownership, or at least a steady, steep rise of the magnitude achieved in the years immediately following World War II. Fore-casts based on census data suggest that current policies will leave us far short of any such goal—that the nation's home ownership rate will increase only to 67.5 percent by the year 2000. But the pace could be accelerated dramatically, as the Department of Housing and Urban Development (HUD) reported in 1994 after analyzing the barriers of affordability and discrimination. HUD projected that if those two barriers could be eliminated, the national home ownership rate in 2000 would reach 85.2 percent.[4]

Do more families want to own homes? Yes, and the data indicate that the desire is usually serious, persistent, and deeply felt. Can we eliminate the barriers? Yes, if we have the political will to live up to the ideals of the nation's founders. And do we have the economic means to help more people achieve their dream? I believe the preconditions for a major expansion of home ownership are already in place; it is up to us to make the most of the opportunity.

Five major forces now at work offer a unique opportunity for a major increase in home ownership during the next decade. Some are more influential than others, but all contribute to a powerful momentum for change.

First, we have transformed the way we finance home buying—the mortgage system—from an industry that is almost exclusively dependent on depositors to one that is investor-based. Consequently, there is practically no ceiling on mortgage growth—the availability of capital to finance home ownership is virtually unlimited. More important, the system no longer transfers interest rate risk from home owners to potentially vulnerable depositories like savings and loans, which have limited risk-management tools to deal with changes in interest rates. Instead, international capital markets now assume the risk, and these are superbly well equipped to evaluate potential performance as they invest in securities backed by mortgages. A bank, a mortgage company, or a thrift will originate a mortgage, approve the application, and grant the loan. But the originator seldom holds the mortgage until it is paid up, or for any appreciable length of time.

The mortgage is sold to the secondary market. That market, led by Fannie Mae, the federally chartered company of which I am chairman and CEO, holds many mortgages at different interest rates, purchased over a long period of time. The secondary market both spreads and minimizes risk. It also shifts the risks to investors by issuing securities backed by mortgages; the investors who buy them assume the risks in exchange for a healthy rate of return.

The secondary market guarantees the investor timely payment of mortgage principal and interest. It manages the risks inherent in the mortgage system by imposing carefully crafted underwriting standards and dispersing the risks on a national basis, across regions, evening out the effects of local recessions and booms. The development of the secondary market is a primary reason for the expansion of home ownership to date—and a primary force for further expansion in the years ahead.

The second significant force in the housing market today is greater affordability, with prices no longer seemingly rocketing out of sight. This is a recent development. Although interest rates continue to fluctuate, home prices are rising only modestly. In addition, the housing financing system is expanding the availability of low down payment mortgages to help people overcome the most significant barrier to home ownership—the up-front cash required not only for a down payment but also for closing costs. Each year, the Joint Center for Housing Studies of Harvard University issues its *State of the Nation's Housing* report. In 1994 the report calculated, "Assuming a 20 percent down payment requirement and typical closing costs, the cash required to purchase the representative starter home in 1993 was a formidable $14,036. Together, down payment and closing costs represented 58.5 percent of first-time buyer income."[5] That's beginning to change, as federally guaranteed and privately insured mortgages significantly reduce down payment and cash requirements for first-time home buyers. The potential for the private mortgage market to extend low down payment lending to more and more borrowers is very real, and it is one of the most realistic ways to expand home ownership.

The third force for change is technology, which will also have a positive impact on affordability. Technology will bring one of the most paper-intensive processes in the world today—the origination and documentation of a mortgage loan—into the twenty-first century. Using technology to simplify the application, information-gathering, and approval process for a mortgage will substantially reduce consumers' cost in securing a loan.

Technology also plays a role in the fourth potential force for change—vigorous enforcement of laws against lending discrimination. If we measure a society by its deeds as well as its words, then we can no longer tolerate a system of mortgage credit that only works for some of the people. We have the laws; we need the will to focus and to act—to prosecute those who discriminate while launching new efforts to eradicate both overt and subtle forms of discrimination at every step of the home-buying process. With increasingly sophisticated technology, regulators will be able to track and monitor lending practices and move aggressively and effectively to open the front door of home ownership to all who qualify.

The fifth force for change is the demographics of population growth in the United States. The population is aging as well as becoming more diverse. By the year 2000, nearly 30 percent of the people living in America will be minorities. Nearly 25 percent of all households will be headed by minorities. More immigrants will come to the United States in the 1990s than at any time since the first decade of the twentieth century. Most immigrants regard a home as the most important investment and claim that they can make in their new homeland. All evidence points to minorities and immigrants as being unusually intent on home ownership—and especially willing to sacrifice to achieve this dream.

As we move toward the year 2000, these five powerful forces can converge to bring this half century's second great increase in home ownership. This book focuses on a strategy to convert that prospect into a brick and mortar and wood reality.

The change this can bring will be vast and peaceful. And as it happens, it will be most visible, at a day-to-day level, in many individual actions—literally millions of them—that will make people's lives and standards of living very different than they otherwise would have been.

In an America shaped by a new home ownership strategy, millions of families who never owned a home, or never thought they could, will join the ranks of home owners. Those who are looking to own a home will work in cooperation with the real estate and mortgage industries to find a way to afford their dream. Lending institutions will actively reach out to prospective buyers, making mortgage financing more accessible and less expensive. No one who applies for a mortgage will be rejected out of hand; everyone will be put on a path of home buyer education to show them how to get "yes" for an answer. The mortgage industry will be the model of diversity. Distressed neighborhoods and inner cities will be stabilized as home ownership gives people a greater stake in their community; this can and will mean higher property values, a lower crime rate, better schools, and improved infrastructures, from streets to parks to shopping areas. Minorities will own homes at the same rate as whites with similar financial resources. Minority entrepreneurship will flourish, bringing new jobs, as one of the most effective avenues of capital accumulation—home ownership—opens up to so many who have been locked out before.

There are few other courses we could take or policies we could pursue that would do as much to strengthen families, communities, and the nation as a whole. So much of our identity, so many of our hopes, are contained in the ambition to own our own homes. From the start, for Americans, a home has been more than another asset; it has been a motivating idea, a nearly universal goal, the most individual of possessions and the most shared of American dreams.

1

Home Ownership and the American Dream

It was Franklin D. Roosevelt who first spoke of the United States as "a nation of home owners." But he was not the first, or the last, president to see owning a home as central to the American character. The aspirations and yearnings of generations of Americans have prompted political leaders on all sides to articulate this ideal and promote policies to help make it real. In the 1920s, Republican president Calvin Coolidge declared, "No greater contribution could be made to the stability of the nation, and the advancement of its ideals, than to make it a nation of home-owning families."[1] In the 1990s, Democratic president Bill Clinton added his voice to the presidential chorus: "Throughout the life of our nation, nothing has been more important as a building block . . . than home ownership."[2]

Political leaders may extol and prod, enlighten and encourage, but in the end, people must be convinced that buying a home matters to their family and their economic future. Millions of individuals have to make the choice—and possess the means—to buy a home. Important questions emerge. First, why do people want to own their own home? Second, what does home ownership contribute to the individual and the economy? And third, how does home ownership shape the nation's political and civic culture?

Why Own a Home?

Pipes burst and you have to phone the plumber. The roof leaks and you call for repairs. The lawn sprinklers can't be turned off. The kitchen floods. The basement mildews. The satisfactions of owning a home—a sense of place, permanence, security—are powerful, but so are the frustrations. Owning a home requires patience and resources. Despite the difficulties, almost all home owners grin and bear it—because they are *owners*, and that means something. Potentially, it means many things. Years of research have revealed a range of reasons.

In a 1947 survey by sociologist Irving Rosow, the number one motivation for wanting to own a home was family pride.[3] Number two was security, both the reality and the symbolism of a stable location. Number three was psychic security—a home provides a private sanctuary where people can in effect be their own boss. Other reasons included status and prestige, neighborhood environment, financial achievement, and family tradition. The desire to own a home, it seemed clear, was deeply ingrained in the popular culture.

Another 1947 study, by Henry McCulley Muller, listed several variations, but the motivations were fundamentally the same.[4] Security was again at the top of the list—but more specifically, security in old age was stressed. Next came a higher status in the community and a better educational environment for children. There were also civic reasons—a belief in private property and the assumption that owning a home makes people better citizens. The Muller survey also cited a variety of financial reasons: a home is a good investment; wanting one is an incentive to save; buying one is a means to improve one's credit standing; owning a home is a way to be independent of landlords; owning a home gives people a valuable asset to leave to their children.

What is most interesting about these surveys, conducted nearly five decades ago, is how little things have changed since then. In a

1993 Fannie Mae survey, 41 percent of respondents answered that security was the single greatest intangible benefit of home ownership. Eighteen percent cited "family values." Purchasing a home ranked second only to getting married—36 percent to 49 percent—as one of the "most important decisions" in a person's life.[5]

The pull of home ownership has been especially powerful for black Americans, despite (or perhaps because of) the fact that for so long home ownership has been markedly less attainable for minority families. In their wonderful book *Having Our Say: The Delany Sisters' First 100 Years*, the 102-year-old Delany twins, daughters of South Carolina slaves, tell a poignant and inspiring story of their struggle to do something that should have been simple—buying a house when they clearly could afford it. In 1957, their brother Hap wanted to buy a house in Mount Vernon, New York, where there were no black home owners. Bessie Delany writes:

> You know, the white real estate agents found excuses not to show him houses in certain neighborhoods, things like that. So do you know what Hap did? He *built* a house. He just went and bought a piece of land right smack in the middle of the nicest white neighborhood, and before the neighbors could figure out what was happening, they were pouring the foundation.
>
> Hap had some trouble for a while, after they moved in. More than once, some white folks cut the tires on his Cadillac. But what those folks didn't understand was that Hap was a Delany, and the harder they tried to push him out, the more he dug in his heels. But his experience did not discourage Sadie and me from moving there. We figured, Why shouldn't we live where we want to?
>
> The first time I answered the door at our house in Mount Vernon, it was some white lady from Welcome

Wagon and she went on and on about this and that and then she said to me, "And be sure to tell the owner . . ."

And I said, "Lady, I have news for you. I am the owner."

Well, she about dropped dead.[6]

The Delanys worked hard—and were tough enough to face down the bigots—in order to buy a home. They overcame barriers that frustrated many other minority families. In that sense, they were pioneers. They were typical, however, in their deep desire to own their own home. That desire cuts across all racial and economic lines and gives brick-and-mortar substance to the notions of achievement and aspiration in American life. In a 1989 Roper poll, respondents ranked home ownership as the number one component of "the good life." Moreover, 75 percent of renters in the poll wanted to buy their own home. Even in the midst of a recession and a decline in real estate prices, a June 30, 1991, *New York Times* survey found that 84 percent of people agreed that buying a home is the best long-term investment in America.[7]

The Social Benefits of Home Ownership

Even in a nation in which many people move each year, planting roots is an ideal with nearly universal appeal. The neighborhood is where most Americans experience community, even when they're not at all conscious of being involved. It's where most children go to school, make friends, and first play ball. It's where we usually shop, worship, walk, and chat. In the impersonal 1990s, a "nice neighborhood" clearly is one of the most important reasons to buy a home. In survey after survey, people say it gives them "a feeling like [they] belong."[8] A home of one's own in a neighborhood that is a place of one's own: what else provides such a sense of stability?

The vision may often fall short, but it clearly reflects reality. The children of home owners are 15 percent more likely to stay in school, even if their parents' income is low. They are 2 to 4 percent less likely to have children of their own before the age of 18, and they are also less likely to be arrested.[9]

In his classic work *The Levittowners*, sociologist Herbert Gans profiled the new home owners in a postwar New Jersey community, one of the nation's first planned suburban developments.[10] He found that their lives had been literally changed, especially the lives of those who had been renters. The community was founded by New York builder William Levitt, who was just trying to sell houses; but his customers obviously bought something more. More than half of them became more active in community organizations after moving to Levittown. Almost half of the former renters went to church or synagogue more often.[11] This remains generally true in the 1990s: home owners are 35 percent more likely to attend religious services.[12]

A home in America involves and expresses a set of values, a sense of belonging and belief. That most American of poets, Walt Whitman, wrote nearly a century and a half ago that "A man is not a whole and complete man unless he owns a house and the ground it stands on."[13]

There have been occasional dissenters who've questioned the value of home ownership. Just as the postwar housing boom hit, one critic assailed pro-ownership surveys as flawed exercises in self-delusion. He scoffed at data from the Depression era that purported to find positive attitudes about home ownership even among those who had endured financial distress or bankruptcy as a result of owning a home: "Our American culture holds individuals responsible for their mistakes, and it is natural for them to keep trying to persuade themselves that they are getting satisfaction out of what they do. . . . Undoubtedly some respondents who had unfortunate home ownership experiences answered the question defensively with 'glad I own.'"[14]

Just three years later, another social scientist went so far as to question the relevance of his own research findings on the attitudes

of owners and renters toward home ownership. Ignoring the signif-
icance of his own data, he instead reiterated his own preconcep-
tions about home ownership: "Because the findings reported here
can be used as evidence in favor of home ownership, the writer
wishes to state explicitly that his own bias lies in the other direction and includes the belief that we have already exceeded the optimum proportion of home ownership in most metropolitan areas."
Yet he found that a far higher percentage of people than that "optimum proportion" would suggest wanted to own a home: 73 percent
of renters in the Minneapolis area wanted to own a home, and over
91 percent of both renters and owners thought that families should
own their own home.[15]

In essence, their argument was that people don't know what's
good for them, that the academics know better. That attitude is
echoed today by economists who insist on classifying home ownership as a form of consumption, not investment or savings. They
would rather have people rent and then, for example, buy stock or
certificates of deposit, foregoing the leverage they would get from a
mortgage. This analysis usually concludes with the suggestion that
government abandon policies that encourage and assist home ownership—in particular, the home interest mortgage deduction. The
irony, of course, is that this would mostly give more money to the
government, not to people so they could invest it.

Some of the earlier, post-Depression academic analysis of home
ownership reflected an honest concern with old-style mortgage bal-
loon payments that could push people over the financial brink. But
then and now, there are other, underlying themes among opponents
of greater home ownership.

For example, in an era of home building and home buying, people vote with their feet—or, in the case of postwar America, with
their cars. They move to the suburbs; they ignore the urban plan-
ner's injunction that it's better, on rational grounds, to live in "the
well-integrated functionally-arranged community planned on the

English model."[16] People prefer decentralization, a home with a yard, even a long-distance commute.

Home ownership, I suspect, is deeply rooted in America's historic individualism. This is proving to be another place where the people and the markets are smarter than the many so-called experts: in the cyber era, as computers free more and more workers from the daily trek to centralized offices and as small businesses in scattered locations become the greatest source of new jobs and new growth, suburbs may make more economic sense than their critics ever imagined they could.

Suburbs have enabled families of moderate means to take out reasonable mortgages and purchase a home with a lawn. As events were confounding the conventional criticism of home ownership in the late 1940s, one academic noted that what was "most destructive to some academic formulations" was that the most common complaints among home owners concerned the age and size of their houses, not the "immobility of location and investment" that critics had theorized to be the main problems facing home owners.[17] People wanted more home, not less. In one survey, nearly 84 percent of home owners expressed satisfaction with their living conditions, versus less than 50 percent of renters. Even more remarkably, among people at the same social and economic level, home owners were more satisfied than renters. Home ownership was a value that cut across all the usual divisions.[18]

In fact, buying a home is not only a financial investment (the greatest one most families make), it is also an investment in the stability of a family—and consequently the health of a society.

Most of us fall between the extremes of the longtime neighborhood fixture and the youthful transient. But almost all who buy are more likely to remain in a community than those who only rent. Home owners tend to be better informed about their school system, the responsiveness of the police force, local government, taxes, and parks. They are more likely to get involved with a community group or the local PTA, perhaps even to organize petitions or protests, support local charity drives, or pay attention to local candidates.

Research has consistently pointed to a wide difference in stability between owners and renters. One study spanning twenty years, from 1925 to 1945, surveyed utility bills in Riverside, California. Sixty percent of the home owners surveyed had lived in the same residence for the past five years, while only 15 percent of the renters had stayed put.[19] The postwar result was predictable: as the nation's home ownership rate soared after World War II, Americans increasingly became a people who literally stayed at home. Between 1940 and 1960, the percentage of people who moved in any five-year period dropped from 59 percent to 49 percent. Ownership was up by 50 percent in this period: three-fifths of Americans had a home of their own, and more than half of Americans were now staying put.[20] One sign of the ubiquity of the suburban ethic was that *On the Road,* one of the most famous novels of the 1950s and the bible of the Beatniks, expressed its sense of rebellion with a title that seemed the antithesis of the American dream of home ownership.

Similar research on Rhode Island residents at the end of a very different decade (the 1960s) confirmed the abiding role of home ownership in creating and maintaining stability.[21] This research also suggested, however, that home ownership may not be an altogether benign reality—that the process of buying and selling a house involves much greater costs and risks than rental transactions. In effect, at closing the home owner is economically bound to a fixed location. There probably is some economic truth to this, but the overwhelming conclusion of most research is that people not only want to own a home but, after owning one, want to keep it or move up to one that's better. Despite the critics, home owning is one of those rare things that actually is as American as apple pie. It is, has been, and seems likely to remain an inherent part of our national character.

Civic and Political Effects of Home Ownership

If home ownership helps to define us as a people, then it inevitably shapes the nation's civic and political landscape. One assumption (the prevailing one) is that those who buy a home tend to become more conservative politically. That may be good or bad, depending on your political perspective, but it is an idea reinforced and popularized during the great postwar housing boom.

In one of the first elections ever held in Levittown, New Jersey, an attractive Republican novice—the quintessential suburban man—defeated a veteran Democratic politician. And, in fact, there was a shift under way: 16 percent of Levittown's new owners had shifted parties, but only 10 percent of Republicans switched, compared to 44 percent of Democrats. Most of the Democratic switchers became self-identified Independents, people who said they "voted the man, not the party." The shift, of course, could go both ways: in Levittown's next election, the Republicans lost by a wide margin.[22]

Perhaps the more powerful pull among the new home owners was class, not party: they could make their own choices; they weren't bound to a ward boss, an immigrant culture, or a city machine. They had stepped out on their own, and no one else and no tradition would tell them how to vote. It was a different world, and it seemed to demand a different politics—less a movement from one side to the other than a chance to stand in the middle and look all the candidates over. It was the natural political posture of those who, for the first time in their lives, could walk out into their own front yard and think of themselves not only as owners, but as suburbanites.

More recent research reinforces the notion that greater home ownership brings more than a switch in party allegiance. A study of the 1976 and 1980 presidential elections, after factoring out variables like age, education, income, race, and socioeconomic status,

concluded that home ownership does not make people more conservative, just more independent. The authors argued that it may
be the case that people's fundamental political orientation is largely
established by the time they buy a home. Buying a home may loosen
that orientation, but not reverse it. Only one group, blue-collar
workers, showed a real change in partisan allegiance. The longer
they lived in their own home, the more likely they were to vote for
a Republican presidential candidate and to identify with the conservative end of the political spectrum.[23]

With rare unanimity, politicians say they favor home ownership.
But on the whole, there is no "home owner vote" in America. Public policy decisions affect issues like the price of homes, and that
reality is a central theme of this book. But most political decisions
are too incremental or too diffuse in their impact to mobilize individual home owners and enlist them behind a particular candidate
or cause. In the political dialogue, there is little or no explicit dis-
sent about the social value and economic benefits of owning a
home. Even in times of apparent ideological clashes, this at least
has been a common ground in American politics. As long as that
continues, why would home owners coalesce politically? As one
observer writes of recent decades, "Their political victory has not
been in doubt."[24]

In short, the nation's founders, and generations of leaders since,
have prized and pursued home ownership as a national goal; contemporary politicians follow a path already well trod. Meanwhile,
the percentage of home owners in America continues to rise. This
very American consensus has dulled the potential cutting edge of
home ownership issues. It also implies, however, that if the leaders
of one political party ever come to be perceived as "anti–home
owner," the political landscape could be transformed overnight by
the voting power of a home owner revolt. We have seen such upris-
ings intermittently, at the state and local level, usually around the
issue of property taxes. The national taxpayer revolt that now spans
an entire generation began in 1978, when California home owners

passed Proposition 13, putting a permanent lid on property tax increases. So, home owners do vote differently—at least sometimes. And they even vote somewhat differently in partisan terms: they vote more Republican. But the research indicates that home ownership itself is not the decisive variable in that difference.

In 1976, in a very close election, 52 percent of home owners voted for Republican Gerald Ford, while 48 percent selected Democrat Jimmy Carter—almost the exact reverse of the national results. In 1980, 54 percent of home owners voted for Ronald Reagan and 38 percent for President Carter. In contrast, only 39 percent of renters voted for Ford in 1976, while 61 percent chose Carter. Again in 1980, only 40 percent of renters voted for the Republican, while 50 percent went Democratic.[25]

In ideological terms, 42 percent of home owners chose the conservative label in 1976, and just 20 percent viewed themselves as liberal. The results were similar in 1980: forty-six percent conservative and 23 percent liberal. For the nation as a whole, in both years, the ideological balance was a little more even, because renters were more liberal than conservative, if only by a small margin. Both those who owned and those who rented included a substantial group of moderates.

So why isn't a nation of home owners bound to become a nation of Republicans? After reviewing voting patterns and ideological identification, the study took into account other variables that affect political outlook—age, race, and income—and found that for the 1976 and 1980 elections, home ownership as an independent factor "had no systematic impact on political orientations."[26]

There is, of course, the separate question not of how people vote but whether they vote at all. The 1993 *Fannie Mae Housing Survey* found that 61 percent of home owners say they vote in "nearly all" local elections, compared to only 35 percent of renters. The earlier data from 1976 and 1980 yielded similar results: home owners were more likely to vote, both in primaries and general elections. But again, is home ownership a cause of better citizenship, or is it merely a coincidence? This time, when the variables are factored out, the answer is different. Owning a home has an independent positive effect on people's propensity to vote.[27]

Home Ownership as an Economic Goal

A person's political status is one thing, his or her economic quite another. The economic consequences of home ownership are more pronounced and, arguably, more profound. Home ownership is not only a powerful index of economic and social status; it is also a vital path of social mobility. Owning a home generally leads to greater capital accumulation; it is a hedge against inflation and an engine of equity accumulation. This is truest for low- and middle-income families, since a home simultaneously represents their major consumption item and their largest form of savings. On average, owning a home accounts for close to 50 percent of family wealth for those in lower income brackets.[28]

Home ownership has the potential both to create and to spread wealth. Building a million new single-family houses in a year directly employs three million people in construction and related industries; it also supports jobs in real estate, banking, insurance, and legal and commercial services. Altogether, it accounts for nearly four and a half million jobs—4 percent of all U.S. employment and tens of billions of dollars in wages and public revenues.[29] Home building alone, without even counting home improvements and sales of existing homes, is the seventh-biggest industry in the nation.

Yet the economic impacts of home ownership on society can't be measured solely in material terms. A home is not just property; it gives people their own stake in a certain kind of society. Capitalism is stronger when more members of society have their own piece of capital. Friedrich Engels's 1872 book *The Housing Question* sounded the Marxist warning against the lure of real estate. It was, in a sense, a remarkably farsighted work, forecasting a society in which the majority of people would think of themselves as part of the home-owning class, not the working class. Engels believed home ownership would fragment the working class as a political force, and he wanted a mobile, increasingly alienated, potentially revolutionary force. "For our workers in the big cities," he wrote, "freedom of movement is the first condition of their existence, and land ownership could only be a hindrance to them. Give them their own houses, chain them once again to the soil, and you will break their power of resistance to the wage cutting of the factory owners." Engels showed particular disdain for mortgages, which he believed would have the effect of "chaining the workers by this property to the factory in which they work."[30] Subsequent Marxist writers have argued—correctly—that home ownership increases the appeal of the status quo, that it furthers the "ideological integration of the working class [into] the dominant ideology."[31]

Engels's vision was half right: wages went up, not down—and the proceeds helped finance a revolution in home ownership. Workers acquired equity and capital; home ownership proved to be the great counter to alienation, a development that the Marxists both predicted and feared.

But the rise in home ownership has tapered off as more and more working Americans find themselves effectively priced out of the home-buying market. Economists like Barton Smith and Zahra Saderion argue that this is not primarily the result of rising home prices. They contend it is largely a labor market problem, not a housing market problem: real wages have stagnated on average and have actually fallen for many, and thus it has become harder for anyone to buy a home. Smith and Saderion point to the alienation felt by those who have been left out: "Frustration is greatest right now for households whose economic status falls just short of supporting homeownership. For this group, the prospects of home-ownership seem to be deteriorating because their real incomes and their share of national income continue to decline."[32]

Home Ownership and the American Dream

"The housing numbers tell us where much of our money has gone, what social choices we have made, and what we have come to believe," writes Adam Smith in *Paper Money*.[33] The numbers currently tell us that 65 percent of American families want to own their homes *and* have achieved that dream. And it is a dream, the greatest common dream of generations of Americans. As Kenneth Jackson puts it, "[The] isolated household became the American middle-class ideal, and it even came to represent the individual himself."[34] To me, a more accurate word is *individual*, not *isolated*. Although a home is often the result of mass production and design, to the home owner, it is unique and personal. It is, in many ways, a statement about who people are, about their hopes, achievements, and family values.

The rise of the suburbs is a story of individualism cast in the context of a new kind of community. While we wish to live with or at least relatively near one another, we Americans don't want to be beholden to others. We generally want control over a lawn, a garden, the color of our walls. Renting, by definition, limits this control. A private dwelling appears to be a nearly universal aspiration. And that aspiration can be best fulfilled, for the greatest number, in the suburbs. Herbert Gans calls the suburbs a physical expression of the desire for "individual and familial autonomy."[35]

A specific ideal of home ownership is expressed by the suburbs, but the reality is not geographically confined. Nearly 120 million people, or 48 percent of Americans, live in suburbia.[36] It is the most popular choice for home owners, but it is not the only choice. In fact, when a recent Gallup poll asked Americans what kind of place they would *like* to live in, 34 percent said a small town, 24 percent chose a suburb, 22 percent a farm, and 19 percent a city. As architects Andres Duany and Elizabeth Plater-Zyberk wrote when they saw these results, "One hardly needs an opinion poll to discover the allure of towns. The market reveals it. Americans have shown over and over again that they will pay premium prices to live in the relatively few traditional towns that remain, places such as Marblehead, Massachusetts, Princeton, New Jersey, and Oak Park, Illinois."[37] My hometown of Benson, Minnesota, with a population that has never exceeded four thousand, has a home ownership rate that has always surpassed the national average.

Some of the experts say towns are the most desired housing destinations; others argue that Americans increasingly prefer even more dispersed suburban settings. This is an issue where almost all views are right, at least to a certain extent, since they come from a diverse population of 263 million. Home buyers make different choices based not only on finances but on personal interests and upbringing. There is no doubt that federal and local policies shape the range of choices available. The general effect has been to expand the range of choice: there are many ways for a family to own a home, from a single-family dwelling in the suburbs to a purchased apartment in a city, a house in a small town, a town house, a co-op, or a condominium.

Whatever the form, home ownership offers one of the classic benefits of capitalism: individuals acting out of self-interest tend, in the aggregate, to benefit the community. In 1776, Adam Smith, author of *The Wealth of Nations*, taught us that the baker does not sell us bread out of benevolence but rather out of self-interest. Similarly, neighbors each look out for their own home and, together, for the neighborhood as a whole. The invisible hand also works in the economy of a neighborhood, street by street. In short, families that own make for communities that are stronger; they have a social and economic self-interest in improving the place where they live and in acting to prevent deterioration. One reason for this, but only one, is that they live in the same place longer; short-term renters are looking ahead, to a different place and time.

Home owners "have a financially-footed, general bias toward social stability." Like any investor, they want a safe investment environment. "Neighborhood life not only affects [home owners] socially but also economically, and this economic bind may create a further impetus to local social interaction."[38]

Americans want to own a home. They believe it's a sensible and maybe even indispensable investment; they see it as an important goal and, for most, their most important single asset. But at Fannie Mae, we're also aware that a hefty majority of people believe that the present system doesn't work well for prospective home owners. The 1994 *National Housing Survey* reports that 60 percent of people said the banking system "works well most of the time," and 43 percent offered the same verdict about higher education. But only 35 percent gave a similar rating to the process of home buying, a confidence level only slightly ahead of the level for public schools.[39]

But a potential home buyer's confidence rises with experience and information. Renters who are actively planning to buy a home have a confidence level eight points higher than those who aren't. The total is 14 points higher among renters knowledgeable about real estate terms.[40]

One fundamental step toward greater home ownership is plugging the information gap. Thirty-three percent of renters say that "not knowing how to get started" is a major obstacle to buying a home, just behind insufficient funds for a down payment and closing costs, and inability to find a home people like that they can afford or a neighborhood where they feel confident about investing in a home. In fact, among renters somewhat likely to buy a home, not knowing how to get started is a more serious obstacle than finding the right neighborhood.[41]

There are Americans who don't want the burdens of home ownership or don't have the economic capacity to handle it. There are others who are in transition periods, coming out of college, moving from job to job, recently divorced. Thus the temporary nature of renting has real advantages for some families and individuals. But one traditional reason not to own has lost most of its relevance: increasingly, people no longer regard forming a family as a precondition for focusing on and moving toward home ownership. More single people (certainly more single mothers and fathers, but even many who have no children) are deciding to buy a home.

There are few exceptions, but the prevailing reality is clear: if you ask renters if it is their goal to own a home, over 80 percent answer yes. This may be due in part to a certain ethos in our society—"that's what you're supposed to do if you're an American." Some renters don't ever really intend or even want to buy. But factor in all the data: 33.5 million households rent; a large portion of these are headed by people in their twenties, an age group for which there's a dramatically lower incidence of home ownership;[42] large numbers of renters are single and lack the economic resources to buy. After taking account of all that, it's fair to estimate that the optimum achievable home ownership rate in America, according to the preferences expressed by renters, is probably in the range of 75 percent. At the same time, if we could cut the costs of building a house; if we could reshape mortgage products to fit individuals to the maximum extent possible, so that people who can realistically meet mortgage payments can get a mortgage; if we dealt a truly effective blow to racial discrimination, which is still a major factor in mortgage finances, then the equilibrium level of home ownership would also be approximately 75 percent. The reality could and should match the desire.

The home ownership gap is real, and many factors contribute to it. One of the most decisive is that a majority of Americans are unfamiliar with the terminology of real estate transactions. Only 45 percent of adults in the 1994 Fannie Mae survey felt very or fairly comfortable with escrow accounts, title insurance, and loan points. Of people with incomes below $35,000 or without a college degree, fewer than four in ten felt comfortable with real estate terms. Renters don't know what they need to know—or where to find it. To obtain credible information on how to qualify for a home loan or mortgage, more renters said they would turn to friends or relatives than to mortgage lenders or mortgage brokers. The top choice for home loan information was a real estate agent.

For renters, the first stage toward buying a home is to save enough money to cover the down payment and closing costs. When they've done that, their next priorities are to shore up credit records and pay off outstanding debts. It is then that too many hit a wall of unfamiliarity and apprehension. The 1994 *National Housing Survey* concluded, "Once the financial concerns of debt, credit record, and gaining mortgage acceptance are overcome . . . doubts about procedures, a need to find someone or someplace to believe in, a fear of making the wrong decisions characterize Stage Three home buyers."[43]

There's a painful irony in this: many Americans are willing to sacrifice—genuinely sacrifice—to own a home; those with the least seem to appreciate the value of home ownership the most. In 1992, Fannie Mae found that 60 percent of those in the lowest income brackets considered "owning your own home" one of their most important long-term goals, while only 31 percent of individuals in the highest income brackets felt the same way. Twenty-five percent more whites than blacks own homes, yet 71 percent of blacks are willing to take a second job in order to save for a home, versus 53 percent of whites.[44]

The Mortgage Interest Deduction and the Benefits of Equity

Some economists think and talk of equity in a home as savings; others see and treat it as consumption. The one change that could lead all economists to adopt the investment and savings view would be to unlock the equity in homes, to tap its potential to add to the nation's economic growth.

Today there are twenty-four million paid-off mortgages in America, and tens of millions more have been paid down; on average, home owners have between $30,000 and $40,000 of equity just sitting there.[45] Much of it can and should be invested in more productive purposes; it should be an active part of the nation's savings picture.

This is beginning to happen. For example, Merrill Lynch now has a home equity account tied to a brokerage account, which allows an investor to deploy the resources in his or her home up to a certain percentage of its appraised value. These home owners can in effect transfer their home equity into stock or bond purchases or other financial instruments that build the economy. To some extent, the debate among economists about whether home ownership represents savings or consumption has become moot. Innovations like home equity lending and the home equity conversion mortgage let elderly people gradually take the equity out of their home to pay living expenses and make investments. Further financial engineering is likely to mobilize more and more of the presently inactive equity in the nation's homes.

The policy makers and economists who intermittently attack the home mortgage interest deduction tend to ignore not only this possibility but also some important and inescapable realities. Limiting but not eliminating the deduction—say, removing it for only more expensive homes—won't raise significant revenue, because the majority of mortgages are in the $100,000 to $150,000 range. Unless these are hit, the yield will be relatively small. Moreover, if we eliminate the deduction just for mortgages of $400,000 and above, the angry reaction will come not only from the wealthy but also from middle-class home owners who are aspiring to buy a bigger or better home. The very wealthy pay down their mortgages, so there may be little or no addition to tax revenues. If we eliminate the deduction altogether, there will be a flattening out of incentives for owning instead of renting, and a corresponding loss to the social benefits of home ownership. Most fundamentally, repealing the mortgage interest deduction would provoke a sharp and immediate drop in the value of the country's housing stock. There would be less equity, not more.

The most authoritative analysis of this issue estimated that home prices would decline 12 to 15 percent, on average, if the mortgage interest deduction were eliminated.[46] Consider a family with a $100,000 house—all of a sudden, it could be worth just $85,000. If they have a $95,000 mortgage on this house, they would face a devastating instant deficit. And if all home owners experienced a similar drop, the nation would face a dramatic drop in existing wealth.

If we eliminate the mortgage interest deduction, we could trigger a real estate collapse like the one we saw in the oil states in the mid 1980s, or worse. Fannie Mae, at one time, owned two thousand houses in Houston. From 1984 to 1992, we owned forty thousand houses in the oil patch, because when there were high loan-to-value mortgages and a steady decline in market values, the mortgages people held became more expensive than the worth of their houses. There were waves of people throwing their keys on the kitchen table and walking out the front door. The legal system offered no way to pursue them. Neighbors would inquire and discover that the owners had gone back to Detroit, or somewhere else, and all of a sudden, as the grass grew up around it, Fannie Mae would have another house in Houston.

Repealing the mortgage deduction would immobilize most of those who are now giving credit—Fannie Mae, the banks, the savings and loans, the insurance companies, all the enterprises that own the instruments of the mortgage finance system. That system is larger than the corporate bond market, the commercial bank loan market, and the consumer loan market put together. To wager it on an economic theory seems reckless as well as needless, especially since home equity doesn't have to be immobilized. The theory also rests on an unstated and unproven assumption, and there is nothing in the economic literature that gives us reason to believe that people would do what the economists say they would do if they weren't investing their money in homes. It may be an even bet, or better, that if Americans didn't put their money into their homes they would simply consume it. Look at the quantity of consumer debt today and the general lack of savings: there is every reason to conclude that money not spent on home ownership would be spent on consumption rather than directed into other forms of saving.

2

Home Ownership in American History

For seventy years, the United States viewed the Soviet Union as its polar opposite. We engaged in "a long twilight struggle" with the Soviets, a conflict that was neither peace nor war. This struggle was responsible, in large part, for the disintegration of the Soviet system. One of the great ideological issues that divided the two sides was property: should it be owned individually or communally (or, more accurately, by the state)?

One of the most memorable television events of the 1950s was the famous "kitchen debate" between American vice president Richard Nixon and Soviet premier Nikita Khrushchev. With a model of an American kitchen as their backdrop, the two men contended over the productivity of their respective economic systems. The underlying dispute wasn't just about which society could produce the most modern kitchen, the first color TV, or the best consumer goods. What the Soviet premier was forced to face in that kitchen was the empirical truth that when individuals are allowed to own property—be it a house, a business, or a factory—the incentives for progress are plainly superior to those afforded by socialism. The undisputed truth was that the Soviet Union, which from its earliest days had outlawed nearly all forms of private property, had become a nation of renters.

Property Rights and American Society

From the start, property as an individual right has been fundamental to the American vision. Home ownership, from town house to farm, was the central image and reality that defined that right when the nation was born. Property rights played a crucial role in early conflicts between the colonies and the British king and parliament and in the eventual battle for independence. To the citizens of the new nation, it was beyond dispute that the right to own property should be explicitly mentioned in its Bill of Rights. To them, liberty and property were inseparable.

Almost one hundred years earlier, when the English Crown grouped New England and New York into a new "dominion" (but permitted no representative assembly), the royal governor of this jurisdiction, Sir Edmund Andros, decreed that all landowning colonists held their property as tenants of the king. He ordered a review of all existing land titles. In April 1689, after King James II was overthrown and William and Mary were installed as constitutional monarchs, a Boston mob arrested Governor Andros and put an end to the short-lived Dominion of New England with a vigorous assertion of their individual property rights.

They cited the mother of all constitutional documents, the Magna Carta, as justification for their stance. From as early as the thirteenth century, the Magna Carta had protected property owners against confiscation without due process. They referred as well to the father of modern political science, John Locke (their own contemporary), who argued that under natural law, private property existed prior to the creation of government, and therefore it was a principal obligation of a just political system to protect natural property rights.

In the years that followed, English Whig politicians, who profoundly influenced colonial thought, virtually equated property ownership with liberty, asserting that private ownership of the land was a bulwark against arbitrary government. In 1721, the Whig writer John Trenchard summed up the argument: "All Men are animated by the passion of acquiring and defending Property because Property is the best support of that Independence."[1] As tensions with Britain rose, "Liberty and Property" became the slogan of protest and then of the drive toward independence. In a 1774 letter, James Madison wrote that he favored "defending liberty and property" against the English: thirteen years later, after independence was won, he carried this conviction to the Constitutional Convention.[2]

Madison fought for the addition of a Bill of Rights with unequivocal guarantees for private property. The Third Amendment prohibited the quartering of troops in a home without the owner's consent, while the Fourth Amendment outlawed unreasonable search and seizure. But it was the Fifth Amendment, best known for protecting citizens against self-incrimination, that contained the most sweeping safeguard of property rights: "[No one shall] be deprived of life, liberty, or property, without due process of law; nor private property be taken for public use without just compensation."

The Fifth Amendment has played a continuing role in protecting home owners in America. In 1795, in *Vanhorne's Lessee* v. *Dorrance*, the Supreme Court held that "the right of acquiring and possessing property, and having it protected, is one of the natural, inherent and inalienable rights of man. . . . The preservation of property . . . is a primary object of [the] social compact."[3] In 1798, Justice Samuel Chase cited the Fifth Amendment in *Calder* v. *Bull*, when he stated that no legislature can "violate . . . the right of private property."[4]

More than a century later, in 1917, the Supreme Court ruled unanimously in *Buchanan* v. *Warley* that the city of Louisville could not enact an ordinance preventing black people from buying homes in white neighborhoods. Justice William Daly wrote, "Property is more than a mere thing that a person owns. It is elementary that it includes the right to acquire, use, and dispose of it."[5] The Supreme Court has upheld a number of environmental regulations that also restrict certain property rights, but the Court, like the Constitution, draws a clear line. In 1994, in a case where a local government was forcing a store owner to give away land, build a bike path, and make other general-purpose improvements in order to obtain a building permit, the Court ruled that the local government's land-use restrictions were not proportional to the public interest. The community has rights, but the individual has a fundamental right to private property.

For the nation's founders, this was not an accident of history or just an article of received faith. It was rooted in the very conception of a free society. Thomas Jefferson, relying on Locke, argued that widespread ownership of private property was crucial to a stable republic. It gave people a stake in the system, a personal identity that conferred an individual independence. People were naturally free, but they were more vested in that freedom and better able to protect it if they owned real property. Jefferson believed this so strongly that he advocated that every adult citizen receive an appropriation of fifty acres of land. He opposed accomplishing this by expropriating land from the wealthy; he remained committed to the property rights of existing owners as well. Rather, he viewed the expansive territories of the new nation as the source of this potential democratic bounty. America was a fortunate continent, an ideal place for a free society and a republicanism sustained by widespread distribution of land.[6] (At that time no one objected to the fact that this idea ignored the property rights of Native Americans.)

Jefferson's ideas of ownership are woven throughout the fabric of our history. National policy in the early 1880s offered vast tracts of land in the Midwest, and the Homestead Act of Abraham Lincoln's time let settlers claim Western land by simply staking it and living on it, as so many people like my grandmother did in places like Swift County, Minnesota. And as the tide of immigration swelled toward the end of the last century, reformers worried about the impact of millions of immigrant renters in the big cities. They worried that without greater home ownership, America would evolve into a socially divided nation of "haves" and "have-nots." From the start, this nation, conceived from property rights, kept reaching to make them more real, for more people, than any other society in history. This was not only an idea; it was dominant policy from the time of the Revolution, when most people owned their own home and more than 80 percent of the population farmed their own land.

But it didn't start out that way. In 1620, the Pilgrims' Mayflower Compact created the first land titles in the colonies, paving the way for legal recognition of land ownership in the United States. It was the seventeenth-century equivalent of claiming and parceling out property on the Moon; the Indians already there were accorded little claim to this "new" world. Also, few among the Pilgrims were ordained to share in this ownership. The investors in the Mayflower's voyage envisioned a system of indentured servitude, with the new arrivals toiling on company-owned plantations. The settlers soon resisted, and the investors soon learned that individual land and home ownership benefitted everyone. The historian Ray Billington recounts the almost instant transition: "The land system insisted upon by the London capitalists who financed the voyage— labor for seven years on a company plantation—worked so badly that in 1623 the division of land among private owners began. This proved successful; within ten years the colony was completely self-sustaining, with its English backers paid in full and the people prosperous. The Pilgrims' ability to maintain themselves without aid from the mother country impressed contemporaries far more than the religious experiment they were conducting, and encouraged other groups to migrate to the New World."[7]

The Growth of Home Ownership

The colonists' first homes were far grander as an idea than they were in reality. The land was theirs, but the homes were often nothing more than dugouts (six- or seven-foot-deep square pits covered by planks), Indian-style wigwams, or structures covered in bark, with ceiling beams made of saplings. But as soon as they could build more substantial homes, the Pilgrims and their Puritan successors gave us two housing styles that are still with us. The two-room "Cape Cod cottage" consisted of one and a half stories with an attic and a large central chimney. The other type, the half-timbered house, featured upright timber frames filled in with branches, leaves, plaster, or brick. In the early days, such houses generally contained two stories, a central chimney, and two to four rooms.[8]

Of course, housing styles varied from colony to colony and reflected the places the settlers came from. The Dutch in New Amsterdam and Albany preferred brick houses. Swedish colonists at Fort Christina in Delaware built the first log cabins, in 1638. Later, pioneers traveling west would build log cabins because they could be constructed cheaply and easily, often within a week. Quaker town houses in Philadelphia popularized stone construction with heavy walls. In Charleston, South Carolina, "the narrow end of the house faced the street and fronted directly on it. Many homes in the city were the summer homes of plantation owners; others housed a rapidly rising merchant class and a middle class of professionals and skilled workers."[9]

From 1701 to 1749, the population of the colonies more than tripled from 262,000 to a little over a million. Only twenty-six years later, on the eve of the Revolution, the number had nearly tripled again, to 2.8 million people. The high seas had become a highway for immigrants. New Hampshire and Pennsylvania were the fastest-growing areas in the North, while the Carolinas, Virginia, and the newly opened Georgia expanded the most in the South. Then, in another remarkable quarter century, from 1775 to 1800, the overall population of the new nation almost doubled, to 5.3 million. Almost all of its citizens lived east of the Mississippi River.

The new government's housing policies reflected its changing demographics. In early New England, land was granted primarily to organized religious groups, who divided it among their adherents.

Soon, however, authorities began to provide (or, more often, auction) land to merchant groups. These early developers planned townships, lured early settlers with free lots, and then profited by selling the remainder. Developers, especially in the South and the mid-Atlantic states, distributed promotional materials and maintained agents at ports where European immigrants were landing.[10] The poor sometimes simply "found" land on their own and built on it. The property rights of these "squatters" were recognized at the end of the Revolution.

Yet most early legislation on westward expansion forced would-be small farmers to buy their land from speculators. Under the Federal Land Ordinance of 1785, pioneers could buy land from the federal government, but only in minimum parcels of 640 acres, far more than most could afford. The investors who could buy large parcels subdivided them and sold them to pioneers on credit. It's probable that some members of Congress were themselves speculating in land sales, and it wasn't until 1820 that the law reduced the minimum purchase to 80 acres.

The Land Act of 1800 primarily covered what is now Ohio and Indiana. Under the act, the new state of Ohio refrained from taxing buyers of public lands for five years. In turn, the federal government set aside money and land in the state to build schools and roads. Between 1800 and 1811, individuals bought more than three million acres under the Land Act, on liberal terms. People from New England and the South arrived to build homes, and by 1812, a quarter of a million people resided in Ohio, which twelve years before had been the edge of the frontier.

Land development banks borrowed funds in Europe and lent them to people moving west and buying land. The mortgage system was slowly coming into being. But since many people lived on smaller (and often inherited) farms, mortgage lending was not an important business in the early United States. In fact, family and friends were the principal source of mortgage funds for most borrowers until the twentieth century.

In 1831 the Oxford Provident Building Association of Frankfort, Pennsylvania, became the nation's first building society. It also became a model for others like it. At first, organizers intended to dissolve each association after it raised enough funds to finance homes for all its members. But even a historically successful enterprise like mortgage lending did not begin without problems; the first loan made by the Oxford Provident Building Association became delinquent, and another association member had to take over both the debt and the house.

The federal government was coming to recognize the difficulties that confronted cash-poor but eager pioneers. In 1830, Congress expanded squatters' rights under the Preemption Act. This allowed cash-strapped squatters to purchase the parcel they were living on at a minimum price, before a public auction was held, if they had already built a home and improved the land. Before that, squatters often lost both their land and house at public auctions. But the Preemption Act did not end speculators' near monopoly on choice land. Farmers with little savings still found themselves at the mercy of loan sharks when the land they had been working, but never bought, finally came up for sale.

It was also possible to suddenly lose the land you had long thought you owned. Abraham Lincoln probably would have remained a citizen of Kentucky, and history almost certainly would have been different, but for the unreliability of land titles.

The famous log cabin where Lincoln was born in 1809 was located in Hardin County, Kentucky. When Lincoln was seven, his father left the state because every time he tried to buy a farm, he found himself confounded by "a crazy-quilt of overlapping land claims. . . . Uncertainty of title drove many a farmer from the state."[11] The family moved to Indiana, where acreage purchased under the Federal Land Ordinance of 1785 offered a more secure title. Certainty of title came only gradually, at different times and in different places. Title insurance was developed as a response to the problem; it remains a standard today, even though the problem has largely disappeared.

The nineteenth century also brought the rise of the first home ownership interest groups. The term *interest group* didn't have the connotation it does today; these groups focused on the very American idea that owning a home was and should be a central feature of national life. The Agrarian National Reform Association urged workers in urban areas to escape the city and become home owners by "voting" themselves a farm—supporting candidates who would back legislation for free or low-cost land. The interest groups were remarkably effective. First came the Graduation Act of 1854, which allowed land unsold for ten years to be bought at only twelve and a half cents an acre. This set off the covered-wagon migration that took generations of Americans westward, many of them settling in the river valleys and trails along the way.[12]

Then the 1860s brought two great transformative events—the Civil War and the Homestead Acts of 1862 and 1866. The first Homestead Act reversed the defect of the earlier federal land law; the government corrected its error in one region but, in effect, made a new blunder in another. The size of the parcels to be given away under the Homestead Act—160 acres—was too small for the West, just as 640 acres had been too large in the East. Thus speculators moved in to buy up and combine parcels into viable farms and ranches. The historian Ray Billington describes the outcome: "The story of settlement under the Homestead Act was not one of down-trodden laborers rising to affluence through government beneficence, but more often a tale of fraud and monopoly which only ended with seven-eighths of the public domain in the hands of a favored few. . . . Yet although failing to provide 'free land for the homeless' it did make farms available for a sizable proportion of would-be farmers who could not otherwise have become independent producers."[13]

After the Civil War, Congress passed a second Homestead Act, primarily for the benefit of the newly freed slaves; it is a metaphor for the failure of Reconstruction and the rise of segregation. In only four years, the act was effectively ended, after just four thousand black families had received free land. Those charged with administering the act sabotaged it: they worked to keep former slaves on the plantation by allotting only substandard land for black homesteaders. They also set claim costs higher than most former slaves could afford.

Despite its inequities, the original Homestead Act opened up the West. It also opened the way for the mortgage system to evolve into its present form. For example, homesteaders often survived the first hard years by mortgaging their property to secure loans for capital improvements. They learned the power of leveraging, using a small amount of their own capital to control a valuable item. Similarly, today's Americans can borrow against the equity in their homes to finance a small business or pay for their children's college education. Homesteading was a defining step in the creation of America's great middle-class, home-owning society.

The Civil War (or, more precisely, the costs of fighting it) sparked another policy to encourage home ownership that endures to this day. With the war costing a million dollars a day, a financially pressed Congress introduced an income tax in 1862. It was the nation's first income tax—and it included a deduction for interest paid on home mortgages. Real estate taxes were deductible as well. The income tax ended in 1872, but not before setting a precedent for home ownership as a protected form of investment.[14]

A Changing Society

The nation was new, on the threshold of industrialization and vast growth, and punctuated by cycles of boom and bust. As urban populations exploded, the United States experienced its first urban crisis. The problems seemed almost insoluble, but of course they ultimately would be solved—and there were early signs of progress. One of the most promising was an effort to connect private housing to public sewer systems. Without this, American cities, towns, and their surrounding areas (eventually called suburbs) could not have grown as they did, at a pace never before seen in any society, a pace that was essentially unbroken for generations.

The United States began as a rural nation, with only 5 percent of its population in nonrural areas. By 1890, over a third of Americans no longer lived on the farm, and within another twenty years, the number had soared to 45 percent. In 1920, for the first time, a majority of Americans lived in nonrural areas. By 1960, the number was nearly 60 percent. Housing this growing urban population involved considerable difficulty; it was a process marked by innovations, shortcomings, and sudden breakthroughs.

For example, as the nineteenth century neared its end, an inefficient mortgage system and poor governmental control of an expanding and then contracting money supply combined to devastate the ranks of farmers and home owners. It was all part of the Panic of 1893, which fueled the Populist revolt and then the Progressive era. Like the Great Depression, the Panic was some time in coming. Under a surface prosperity, the bubble was beginning to burst. Farmers often carried large mortgages—as they still do—and a financial collapse in 1887 left many of them with no money to service their debt. They were forced to turn to loan sharks, who charged interest rates of between 20 and 40 percent. From 1889 to 1893, eleven thousand farm mortgages were foreclosed in Kansas; one-quarter of those who had owned farms were reduced to the status of tenant sharecroppers. There was a brewing revolt not only against the railroads, which had previously been the target of popular grievances, but also against the nation's entire financial structure. The anger was fierce: "The West, it appeared, was becoming an area of landless peasants where absentee landlords and corporations owned the soil."[15]

One reaction was political—from the call for "free silver" to Theodore Roosevelt's "Square Deal." The other reaction was demographic—an acceleration of the migration from rural to urban

areas. As the tide of immigration mounted, both from other coun-
tries and from the countryside, the cities strained to absorb the
increase. Tenement houses, primitive even by nineteenth-century
standards and often filled with a half-dozen families or more, came
to dominate entire neighborhoods. As the new century dawned,
these conditions increasingly set the stage for government action
to improve both the quality of housing and opportunities for home
ownership.

Between 1895 and 1920, municipalities and states adopted a
host of laws to regulate tenements. The federal government had no
housing policy; in fact, it did less at the beginning of the twentieth
century than it had in the early days of the republic. Then, in 1913,
when Congress reestablished the federal income tax, it also rein-
stated the home interest mortgage deduction. In 1994 alone, the
deduction saved Americans almost $52 billion.[16] The income tax
shaped housing trends in two other important ways. First, it provided for deductibility of property taxes on owner-occupied homes.
Second, the law exempted interest from state and local bonds from
income taxes. The first such bonds were issued after World War I to
help returning veterans buy homes.

As the frontier closed and people decided or were forced to
move to urban areas, the rate of home ownership naturally dropped.
The percentage of American families owning their own homes stagnated and then fell, from almost 48 percent in 1890 to 46 percent
in 1900, 45.8 percent in 1910, and 45.6 percent in 1920. But most
remarkable may have been how small this drop really was. In reality,
more people were buying homes, but because there were also record
numbers of new households forming, the *rate* of home ownership
decreased. In 1905, a million immigrants came to the United States,
followed by 1.3 million in 1907. New arrivals tended to rent rather
than own in the first years after their arrival.

Nevertheless, the rate of home ownership was relatively low
compared to our current rate of about 65 percent. The primary reason was the lack of adequate financing mechanisms to fund hous-

ing purchases. Problems in the mortgage market prevented America from becoming, as it had been in the early days, a majority home-owning nation. Simply put, the mortgage system was a mess. Today we are all familiar with the book of monthly coupons (each for a combined interest-and-principal payment) that mortgage companies and banks send their borrowers, who write monthly checks and send them in with a coupon until the loan is repaid in fifteen or thirty years. In the 1920s, however, most borrowers didn't even make payments on a monthly basis, nor did their mortgages extend for periods of fifteen or thirty years. Often, an entire lump-sum payment of principal was due after three to five years. Interest was due once a year. Moreover, to reduce risk, most loans were limited to a fraction of the home's value, usually 40 percent. To cover the rest of the cost, people had to search for second and third mortgages, which carried effective interest rates as high as 20 percent, compared to 5 to 7 percent for first mortgages.

A system characterized by little bank credit on the one hand and massive imminent borrower liabilities on the other was doomed to collapse. And so it did. In 1933, in the depths of the Great Depression, an astonishing 49 percent of the $20 billion in home mortgage debt in America was in default. Foreclosures averaged a thousand a day.[17] And this time, home ownership did fall—not by a little, but measurably and markedly—and the undeniable cause was the financial crisis, not shifting population patterns. The home ownership rate was 47.8 percent in 1930 and 43.6 percent in 1940. The decline would have become an utter collapse without the New Deal legislation that put a moratorium on mortgage foreclosures.

Both Herbert Hoover and Franklin Roosevelt saw the home mortgage credit crisis as an urgent priority. As commerce secretary in the 1920s, Hoover had always believed that home ownership was a fundamental American aspiration. He prided himself on being a conservative president, but as the downturn took its toll, he decided that this was one area where the federal government had to act. In August 1931 he established a planning committee to investigate "problems . . . in home ownership and home build-ing . . . and removal of influences which seriously limit the spread of home ownership."[18]

The joint chairmen of the planning committee, the secretary of commerce and the secretary of the interior, created twenty-five sub-committees and instructed each to prepare a report for a presiden-tial conference to be held that December. The commission, the committees, and the conference actually made a difference: many of the ideas that emerged from the process became law in the years that followed.

One of the first, in 1932, was the Federal Home Loan Bank Act. It was designed to restore liquidity to the nation's banking system so that banks would lend to potential home buyers, thereby spurring construction, creating jobs, and reducing the 24 percent unem-ployment rate. But the crisis, in both finance and confidence, was too deep. Home owners trying to renew mortgage loans were still being denied, and banks that needed the money to meet pressing obligations of their own still demanded lump-sum principal pay-ments. Many short-term mortgage loans came due at approximately the same time, which intensified the downward spiral: the mounting volume of foreclosed homes for sale by lenders depressed the hous-ing market, leading to even more foreclosures, the failure of more lending institutions, and a near standstill in new construction.

Hoover's intervention was unprecedented, in this area and in others. But here and elsewhere, it was not enough. His successor, Franklin Roosevelt, saw the challenge as fundamental—and fun-damentally related to home ownership. Roosevelt's mind-set was described as follows: "To [him], the Great Depression threatened homeownership and the state itself. Roosevelt perceived the failure of the American economic-political system to protect private prop-erty in the home as a central problem of the Depression. . . . He also believed that the social compact of the early Republic, which Jef-ferson had defined in terms of the yeoman farmer who worked the land he owned, needed to be modernized for the industrial era."[19]

Roosevelt spoke often and powerfully of his commitment to property rights. In the 1932 campaign he called for major financial changes to protect and widen home ownership. In his historic "Forgotten Man" speech to the Commonwealth Club of San Francisco, he sounded this theme: "Every man has a right to his own property; which means a right to be assured, to the fullest extent attainable, in the safety of his savings. By no other means can men carry the burdens of those parts of life which, in the nature of things, afford no chance of labor; childhood, sickness, old age. In all thoughts of property, this right is paramount."[20] In one of his first messages as president, Roosevelt demanded special safeguards for home ownership, lest the country face social and economic instability.

The central problem was that too many people who had the desire to keep their home didn't have the means. They were out of work, or underpaid, or out of savings. To halt the flood of foreclosures and of home owners' being forced to sell as they fell behind on their mortgage payments and property taxes, the Roosevelt administration created the Home Owners' Loan Corporation, or HOLC, one of the early alphabet agencies that characterized the New Deal. The HOLC essentially refinanced troubled mortgages with cash loans and rescued lending institutions by exchanging government-backed bonds for mortgages in default. Eventually, the agency also made direct loans to help people pay their taxes and insurance.[21]

The HOLC's work was not always smooth, but it was sweeping and it left a lasting imprint. From June 13, 1933, to June 25, 1935, when it stopped accepting loan applications, the agency made or assumed just over one million loans, valued at over $3 billion. This was a staggering sum in the 1930s, equal to almost half of one year's federal budget—a figure that would equal over $700 billion today. One out of every ten owner-occupied homes in America—20 percent of all homes with mortgages—was refinanced because of the HOLC. The agency also loaned money for home improvements to 40 percent of all mortgage holders in America.

Originally, HOLC loans had a term of fifteen years. But by 1939, public pressure resulted in the Mead-Barry Act, which extended the term to twenty-five years and sharply reduced the required monthly payment. Finally, in 1951, the HOLC closed its doors and its books, providing a small profit for the taxpayers. The outstanding loans were sold to nongovernmental institutions, which were only too happy to buy them. This all-but-unnoticed event was a proud symbol of a mission accomplished.[22]

The HOLC was Roosevelt's response to rampant foreclosures. But the challenge wasn't limited to helping people keep their old homes; the other issue, more urgent with each monthly unemployment report, was making it possible to build and buy new ones. The National Housing Act of 1934 was designed to stimulate the construction industry, create construction jobs, and restore the availability of mortgages—the very goals that the Hoover administration's Home Loan Bank Board had failed to achieve. The 1934 act had a longer-range purpose as well—to recast the chaotic national mortgage market into a more rational and regular system. The vehicle for this change was the Federal Housing Administration, or FHA, as it would come to be known to generations of Americans, an agency that would encourage lending and over time gather the financial reach and power to standardize mortgage practices nationwide.

The FHA insured the lender against losing money if a home owner defaulted on payments. Over three decades later, a congressional committee summed up its impact: "Consumers buying FHA-aided houses benefitted by being able to obtain home ownership earlier and at lower monthly costs. They also benefitted from the fact that the FHA-aided housing was subject to minimum standards applied to its location, design, materials, and construction methods. Compliance with minimum standards in the case of new housing was obtained through inspections."[23]

The 1934 housing act gave banks the guarantees and confidence to lend again. It gave home owners the chance to obtain a single mortgage covering a large portion of a house's appraised value. It extended the length of mortgages, usually to thirty years, and made monthly amortization of principal and interest a common part of home ownership. But the act accomplished much of this indirectly and gradually, only as its ripple effects were felt over the years.

For example, Title III authorized the FHA to start privately owned mortgage associations to buy and sell mortgages on the secondary market. These institutions would purchase mortgages from many different banks, spreading the risk of default and converting the banks' debt instruments into new liquidity so they could loan again. But then nothing happened for three years. The depressed state of the economy worried potential investors, who in order to participate in this plan would have to commit $5 million to an untested venture. One of the major architects of the New Deal, Jesse Jones, chairman of the Reconstruction Finance Corporation (RFC), wrote later, "We were never able to get anyone to start a mortgage company. Times were so pessimistic that no one would put up money for common stock in such an enterprise. . . . We wanted private investors to own the business, to do the work and make a fair profit. But we couldn't induce anyone to try it."[24]

By 1935 the RFC, which was originally designed to shore up corporate finances, was itself buying up FHA-insured mortgages. It was a stopgap measure designed to recirculate mortgage funds back to potential lenders. But this improvisation had an unintended, if predictable, side effect: now potential investors were reluctant to fund private mortgage associations because of competition from the RFC. The agency was not only already there, it was also operating in a relatively small mortgage market: FHA mortgages insured for repurchase were not available in substantial or certain numbers in the early years, limiting the potential profits of private investors.

The Legacy of the Depression

The Great Depression and the New Deal meant different things to different people, depending on their perspective. Some saw it from the top down, from the perspective of Washington. People like my father, Alfred I. Johnson, saw it from the perspective of a local community, like Benson, Minnesota. He was born just outside of Benson in 1898. He had eight brothers and sisters, all raised on a small farm in Six Mile Grove township. He worked on the farm until he was twenty and then found a job at the town bakery, where he worked at night. He then became a clerk at the Jack Sprat grocery store.

After a period of time my father and his partner, Myron Johnson, bought the Jack Sprat store from another local family, the Lees. The store sold dry goods as well as groceries. Just as they bought it, the depression hit. My father had to become a source of credit, because suddenly there were a lot more poor people in Benson; sometimes they could pay for their groceries, and sometimes they couldn't. He would keep an account of their purchases and basically manage how far he could let them go without paying. My mother, who taught Latin, German, and social studies in the local high school, always remembered him stretching to the limit, and past it. He managed the store this way all through World War II.

Benson, of course, wasn't typical—no place really is. It should have been better prepared to weather the depression; it was, and is, the most stable of stable communities. Benson was a railroad town that had been settled during the 1880s. There was a substantial Irish population around the town, concentrated at the railroad stops four and eight miles out of town in either direction. But Benson itself was heavily Norwegian. When I was growing up, the main Norwegian Lutheran church had two thousand members, because it drew from twenty or thirty miles around; the smaller country churches were merging with the "big" church in town. There was an Episcopalian church that had about twenty members and space for about forty. It was the smallest church I've ever seen. There were a few other churches as well. Whichever one they went to, everybody in Benson went to church.

Benson was also the county seat, so the courthouse was there. As the depression deepened and the New Deal sought to prime the pump and hire the out-of-work, all the town's major recreational facilities were built or rebuilt by the Works Progress Administration (WPA). All of them were owned and run by the school system or the city. There was no such thing as a private club. There was almost no private anything—except for the few restaurants in town, but everyone thought of them, too, as public facilities.

I can't ever remember anybody being excluded from anything for any reason. Benson was egalitarian. I see that again whenever I go home. The people of Benson are more interested in an individual's character, and in the values and ideals that guide one's choices in life, than they are in any external measures of success or accomplishment. They honor honesty, integrity, hard work, and commitment to family and community; they aren't impressed by money or fame.

Benson was the kind of community that pulled together in the depression. But towns like Benson would never had made it through the depression without the New Deal, the WPA, the HOLC, the FHA, and all the rest. Homes would have been lost; communities simply would have disintegrated. Then, suddenly, just when it seemed the worst was over, the recovery stopped and the depression returned.

The economic collapse of 1937 threatened all of the New Deal's progress in employment, public works, and housing policy. The collapse threatened to wipe out the infant private mortgage associations that investors had been so afraid to form; their fears, it seemed, had been vindicated. But the New Deal was nothing if not pragmatic—and Franklin Roosevelt, who so identified with his "home on the Hudson," saw increasing home ownership as essential to the recovery. He directed RFC chairman Jones to investigate founding a permanent government mortgage association whose sole business would be to buy up FHA mortgages on new houses. The banks had to resell their mortgages if they were ever to issue more, Roosevelt believed, and the problem could no longer wait for the private sector to solve it. So a year later, Congress enacted the Federal National Mortgage Association—now known as Fannie Mae.

Fannie Mae began its life in a profoundly different financial world than the one we know today. Before deregulation in the 1980s, the only business of savings and loan associations (S&Ls, or building and loans, as they were often called) was to use their depositors' money for housing loans. The difference between the interest paid to depositors and the interest charged on mortgages provided their profit. This spread resources and risk, but only within the limits of a small community.

A primitive "secondary market" evolved, in which S&Ls with too many mortgages and too little to lend would sell their existing loans at a discount to nearby S&Ls in order to raise cash. But the limited geographic scope of such transactions left some communities with severely limited mortgage funds, even in the best of times. In the 1930s, savings in Minnesota were not used to finance home mortgages in California, although that is essentially what happens all the time today. Back then, in the event of a downturn like the 1937 collapse, conditions rapidly worsened. S&Ls that had formed a secondary market in a limited area faced a domino effect of panic and insolvency as depositors sought to withdraw their funds. The money to repay them wasn't there, of course, nor was it in any nearby S&L.

Jimmy Stewart's classic film *It's a Wonderful Life* told the story in everyday, human terms. George Bailey, the local S&L manager played by Stewart, has to confront an angry mob demanding their deposits back. As they crowd and shout at the teller's window, he stands his ground and explains that the money isn't there. He tells them it's not as if he had the money back in a safe. "Why, your money's in Joe's house . . . and a hundred others. You're lending them the money to build, and then they're going to pay it back to you."

The Roosevelt administration was determined to reinforce that principle, not supplant it. Indeed, as early as 1934, the president proved ready to compromise in order to achieve the paramount objective of secure and available mortgages for ordinary Americans. The S&Ls opposed the original FHA mortgage guarantee program because it threatened to bring on new competition from potential lenders such as insurance companies and commercial banks, which until then had confined their lending largely to the vicinity of their own base of operation. So Roosevelt offered a grand housing bargain: the 1934 law that created the FHA and provided for private mortgage associations also established the Federal Savings and Loan Insurance Corporation to protect S&L deposits.

But when the FHA fell short and the private mortgage associations did not materialize, the thrift industry then opposed the reforms that created Fannie Mae. The S&Ls had their deposit insurance—why would they want or quietly accept a new, government-backed secondary market for mortgages that would be "more sophisticated than any run by the thrift industry?"[25]

Eventually the S&Ls would learn to coexist and then cooperate with Fannie Mae, which in its first year bought $35 million worth of new FHA mortgages. The reforms did not revive the construction industry, but they did stabilize it. The HOLC protected existing home owners from foreclosure, and the RFC, the FHA, and Fannie Mae helped finance new homes—not as many as Roosevelt had hoped, but more than would have been built or purchased otherwise.

Most of all, the New Deal reforms set the stage for the great home ownership revolution that was to come after World War II. The reforms laid the foundations for the national, and eventually international, secondary market for mortgages. Out of the ashes of the Great Depression rose the structures to accommodate the housing and baby booms that followed World War II, which few Americans could foresee in 1940 or 1941. Who knew that the aftermath of a war fought thousands of miles from American shores would transform not only our lives but also where and how we would lead them, in the tens of millions of new places we would call home?

3

The Postwar Housing Boom

America's great boom in home ownership did not come until after World War II. During the war, the government focused the entire society on winning the war. In fact, it pursued policies that actively discouraged the building or buying of new homes. The metal in every nail, bolt, and earth mover was potentially part of a weapon, and that was the priority. The Roosevelt administration, so recently the champion of home ownership, also feared inflation. So in 1943 it instituted rationing and set price controls on a range of goods. The controls led to shortages and direct restrictions on nonessential economic activities such as residential housing construction. Dr. New Deal, as Roosevelt had been dubbed, became Dr. Win the War—and new housing was not part of the prescription.

Ironically, this policy took effect just as the greatest internal migration in American history was beginning. And unlike tires or meat, or a host of other items, it was impossible to buy a house on the black market. As one historian observed, "The one thing that might have tempted law-abiding citizens wasn't available on the black market: housing. War rearranged the population. . . . [Over fifteen million] Americans moved in the early 1940s, half of them to different states. Wives and girlfriends followed servicemen to camps and bases all over the country. Workers migrated from farms and small towns to big cities and out-of-the-way places where huge new factories created instant communities."[1] Where were these people to live? The most that the government would do—or could do—in a time of war was to urge families to take in renters.

The end of the war marked the start of an unprecedented housing boom. Soldiers returned home with marriage and family on their minds. Depression and war had left a shortage of homes to meet the demand. Private builders began a feverish, generation-long burst of home building. Annual housing starts increased from 142,000 in 1944 to 1.95 million in 1950; in the four years immediately following the war, the home ownership rate jumped from 44 percent to 55 percent. And housing starts never fell below 1.2 million a year from the late 1940s to the mid 1960s. The majority of these new homes were owner-occupied residences.[2]

The house I grew up in was one of those residences, and the town of Benson, Minnesota, where that house was located, was the kind of community that I believe so many Americans were trying to create— or re-create—after the weariness of a long depression and the exertions of total war. Benson was a reassuring place. Five of my father's brothers and sisters lived within a block of where we lived. My mother's brother owned the lumberyard down the street. I could walk out on any given day when I was five, six, or ten and within a few blocks literally find twelve cousins and twelve aunts and uncles.

In the years right after the war, when I was growing up, my father's family had a reunion every Saturday night. Even when I was in high school, when I would leave the house to go play a basketball game or go to the movies, my mother would say as I headed out the door, "We're going to be at Bert's tonight" or "We're going to be at Ole's tonight." So when I was finished with the movies, or with my game, I would ride my bike or walk to the house where the family gathering was being held.

The Levittown Phenomenon

America—even the America of the late 1940s and 1950s—wasn't like Benson. It was already too urban and too mobile. But the ideal of a town like Benson was what a lot of Americans, from Boston to Los Angeles, were looking for. They found their dream, or the closest approximation to it, in the suburbs, the focal point of the postwar era's housing boom and its decisive contribution to the nation's way of life.

The first orchestrator of the suburban trend was a New York builder, William Levitt, who "was to suburbs [what] Henry Ford was to the auto. Neither one of them invented it. Neither one of them made any major contribution to the technology of the idea, but both of them popularized it, both of them did it in a bigger way than anyone had done it before."[3]

In a potato field twenty-nine miles from Manhattan, Levitt engineered an assembly line for housing: in this case the workers moved, not the product. Framers, carpenters, and window caulkers completed their task and moved on to the next house. So did workers installing toilets, sinks, and shingles. Twenty years before, no one would have thought of building in this location, so far from the city—or of building in this way. Now both the location and the method were an advantage. At a rate of 150 houses a week, Levittown quickly grew into a thriving suburban landscape of seventeen thousand four-room, Cape Cod–style houses, each eight hundred square feet with a small yard in the front and back. Nationwide, other developers repeated this formula for instant home ownership, as did Levitt himself in Pennsylvania and New Jersey.

Changes in the mortgage system played an essential role in helping veterans afford these houses. In 1944 Congress passed the GI Bill, which set up a Veterans Administration program that offered federal guarantees for returning troops' mortgages. These came to be known as VA loans. In effect, a builder would go to the VA or FHA and state his intention to construct new homes. The agencies would guarantee or insure the mortgages on the condition that the VA or FHA would set quality standards and enforce them with home inspections. Without commitments from the VA or FHA, many builders would not have been able to find the financing to build new houses; thus FHA and VA approval became a practical precondition for receiving an initial construction loan. Because of these requirements, veterans could obtain a good home at a good price and pay for it with a good mortgage.

The FHA and VA programs minimized risk to lenders. By insuring or guaranteeing individual mortgage loans, the federal government left lenders virtually certain to recover their money in the event of a foreclosure. At the outset, the VA guarantee generally covered losses up to a $7,500 ceiling, which was sufficient for most homes built in that era. Drawing on all available programs and resources, the 1946 "Veteran's Emergency Housing Program" helped push housing starts over the one million mark that year, compared to three hundred thousand in 1945.

With both FHA and VA loans available to them, former soldiers could buy a $7,990 Levittown home with a down payment of $90 and monthly payments of $58 a month on a twenty-five-year mortgage. Veterans often slept outside to be first in line for the new houses. The developments also inspired an early preview of today's no-growth movement. The town board of Hempstead, New York, on Long Island, enraged would-be home buyers by restricting its zoning to exclude many Levitt-built homes. Board members said they were concerned about the character of the town. The wife of one veteran told besieged board officials at a town meeting, "It's too bad there aren't more men like Levitt & Sons. . . . I hope they make a whopper of a profit."[4] The board changed its mind.

Suburbs like Levittown reflected the greater society in the United States even as they were changing it. They were new, but they perpetuated and even deepened old patterns of segregation. Each home owner contract in the Long Island Levittown contained a restricted-covenant clause that read, "No dwelling shall be used or occupied by members of other than the Caucasian race."[5] The Levitts were marketing the great American dream, but it was clearly stamped "For Whites Only."

Levittown, Pennsylvania, was typical: it was 100 percent white until August 1957, when a black family moved in. Soon after their arrival, more than two hundred people crowded outside the black family's home at night throwing stones, one of them smashing a picture window. Thus began a campaign of intimidation against the family of William Myers, a college-educated black World War II veteran. It ripped the community apart. Members of the so-called Betterment Committee, formed to keep Levittown white, constantly gathered near the Myers' home. They kept up a constant barrage of insults, driving by the house late at night with their radios blasting, conspicuously displaying Confederate flags on caravans of automobiles, and banging repeatedly on a nearby mailbox late at night. They made threatening phone calls to the Myers family and even to people who had remained neutral. They burned crosses on the Myers' lawn. There were waves of hate literature, and for a period of four nights in September, crowds gathered behind the Myers home and shined bright lights through the windows. But through it all, the Myers family stayed.

They displayed what one writer called remarkable "emotional stamina." Fortunately, Pennsylvania's governor and attorney general had the courage to do their jobs. The governor sent in the state police, and both officials made it clear that any act of violence would be fully prosecuted. Early in the fight, Governor George Leader spoke out: "The stoning of the home of the first Negro family in Levittown is completely alien to the historic principles upon which Pennsylvania was built. . . . Any family has a right to live where it can obtain legal possession, on any street, road or highway in this Commonwealth."[6] The governor's stand encouraged the Citizens' Committee for Levittown, a group formed to oppose the bigots.

Attorney General McBride personally went into court to gain an injunction barring acts of violence or intimidation against the Myers family or any other black family who might seek to buy a home in Levittown. That ended the battle. And though scars remained, over the next three years four more black families and one racially mixed couple bought homes in the Pennsylvania Levittown—and there was no reaction at all. But the battle for housing integration in the rest of America would be long and protracted. It hasn't ended yet.

The Suburbanization of America

In the meantime, the astounding success of the Levittowns and their imitators both signified and spurred the population shift from America's cities to its suburbs. In my home state of Minnesota, the suburb of Bloomington was a sparsely populated town in 1950; ten years later it was filled with fifty thousand people living in single-family homes. Eleven of America's twelve most populous cities lost population in the 1950s, with most of the baby boomers being born in the suburbs. The one exception was Los Angeles. In that era it was hardly a central city in anything but name; essentially it was a collection of suburbs stretching across 451 square miles. The San Fernando Valley, a vast stretch of orange groves and farmland, was largely within the Los Angeles city limits; later it would become the quintessential Sun Belt suburb.

The increase in home ownership following the war fueled unprecedented economic growth. Car sales boomed along with the suburbs; from 1945 to 1965, car registrations soared from 26 million to 72 million. By the mid 1960s, nearly 80 percent of American families owned a car. Nothing like it—the mobility, the autonomy, the spread of wealth—had ever before been seen in world history. The federal government helped create that history with another massive program, the interstate highway system, which also (and not just accidentally) sped the migration from city to suburbs.

The suburbanization of America gradually brought with it another phenomenon—the shopping mall. Main streets and downtowns began losing businesses to this new kind of commercial center, which also became a social magnet. The decentralization of

America widened as manufacturing sites and office parks followed the freeways to the suburbs. Southdale Center, America's first completely enclosed, climate-controlled mall, with neatly stacked rows of stores and restaurants, opened outside Minneapolis in October 1956. The man who later coined the phrase "the malling of America" wrote, "After Southdale it was clear. The mall would be the center of everything for suburbia."[7]

The trend toward home ownership accelerated even more after Congress passed and President Truman signed the Housing Act of 1949. The act committed $500 million more for FHA mortgage insurance. It also gave new life and a broader role to Fannie Mae, the nascent secondary mortgage agency that had been little more than an idea in waiting during the war. Henceforth, Fannie Mae could purchase mortgages for rental and cooperative housing as well as FHA mortgages on single-family homes. The act also permitted the company to buy VA-guaranteed mortgages. Fannie Mae was suddenly deeply involved with helping an entire generation of veterans buy their own homes.

The legislation contained two especially controversial elements—it authorized increased funding for low-rent public housing, and it created a new program to clear city slums and spur urban redevelopment. The House of Representatives passed the measure by a narrow margin of 209 to 204.

Some of the criticism heard during the debate over the act has been proved right over time. Densely concentrated, high-rise public housing is now seen as a blight, not a boon—as government-subsidized vertical slums. Some urban redevelopment has been a powerful revitalizing force but not for the better. Much so-called redevelopment created cold, concrete, seemingly lifeless preserves where there once was a thriving urban life. Still, for all its shortcomings, the 1949 Housing Act and the train of legislation that preceded and followed it, when taken together, had a positive, profoundly transformative impact. The modern conservative who writes under the pseudonym Adam Smith not only concedes this point, he emphasizes it: "In 1920, somewhere around 50 percent of Americans lived in what the 1949 Housing Act would call 'decent housing': 'having indoor plumbing and no dilapidation.' By 1960, 82 percent of the population lived in 'decent housing' and 62 percent owned their own homes."[8] Those statistics represent a legislative and social triumph. The first great wave of social legislation in America saved a bankrupt system, turning it around and creating, in the span of one generation, a high rate of home ownership nationwide. Savers put their money in the banks, the banks lent that money to house buyers, the house buyers paid off the loans—and the government agencies behind the process cost the taxpayer almost nothing.

In 1951, Congress added another incentive for people to own their home by amending the Internal Revenue Code to let taxpayers defer capital gains from the sale of a principal residence. A seller now has two years to reinvest the proceeds in another house (one that is at least as expensive as the house sold) without incurring a tax liability. Americans, already the most mobile people of any industrial society, became even more so: home owners could sell and buy a new residence of greater value and pay no taxes on the gain—just as if they had never moved at all. In 1994 this provision saved home owners $13.8 billion in taxes. In 1999 it will save them $16 billion. Another provision, first enacted in 1964, now permits people over 55 a one-time exclusion on $125,000 in capital gains from the sale of a principal home. Congress decided not to penalize older Americans for moving to a new, less costly residence, allowing seniors to contribute more to their own support. This provision saved seniors $4.7 billion in taxes in 1994.[9]

The Evolution of Fannie Mae

Fannie Mae, revitalized in 1949, was transferred in 1950 from the Reconstruction Finance Corporation to the Housing and Home Finance Agency, which later became the Department of Housing and Urban Development (HUD). For the better part of the next two decades, Fannie Mae was the leader in achieving marketplace acceptance of new government housing initiatives, including the purchase of FHA mortgages for housing in Alaska, mobile homes, elderly housing, and nursing homes. Fannie Mae provided the essential leverage.

In 1954, Congress opened the agency to private shareholders. This was a first step toward the 1968 decision to divide the agency into two separate entities—the Government National Mortgage Association (Ginnie Mae), which as a part of HUD continued to carry out government subsidy and special assistance programs,[10] and Fannie Mae, which became an entirely shareholder-owned, privately managed corporation in the secondary mortgage market. Fannie Mae shareholders paid the government over $200 million to buy the government's remaining interest in the corporation.

The change came just in time for the credit crunch of 1969 and 1970. As a private corporation, Fannie Mae could adapt almost instantly to market conditions. The new enterprise moved rapidly, buying almost half of all new FHA and VA residential mortgages originated during that time. From October 1969 to March 1970, the money Fannie Mae pumped back into the system by purchasing home mortgages accounted for almost half of the increase in funds going into single-family mortgage loans. No single institution had ever before played so dominant a role or become so influential in such a short period of time.

The credit crunch led the savings and loan industry to seek its own version of Fannie Mae, since Fannie Mae served mortgage bankers, not S&Ls. The idea was already a proven success, so Congress established Freddie Mac to serve the S&Ls and altered Fannie Mae's charter to permit it to purchase conventional as well as FHA and VA mortgages. This expanded Fannie Mae's reach: by the end of the 1970s it would push $63 billion into the nation's housing market, nearly tripling the amount it had provided during the previous thirty years. With two major institutions suddenly responsible for such a high volume of mortgages, the inevitable result was greater uniformity in mortgage instruments, which were increasingly written to meet Fannie Mae standards, and greater liquidity in the marketplace. Basically, it was easier to buy, sell, and trade mortgages written in the same financial language.

The 1970 legislation chartering Freddie Mac and expanding the scope of Fannie Mae finally shaped a secondary mortgage market—as originally envisioned in the 1930s—that functioned as a dependable source of funds for home buyers. Over the next quarter century, home mortgages evolved from being depositor-based to becoming investor-driven. Mortgage funds no longer depend on savings from the local community; they are financed nationally and internationally through the capital markets. The risk can now be spread globally, and it increasingly is.

Home Ownership as an Investment

The high inflation of the 1970s made home ownership even more important as an investment, as a hedge against rising prices. A home became more than a place to raise a family; it offered a way to secure its financial future. Home owners borrowed substantial sums of money to buy a house, but they paid the mortgage back in less valuable "inflated" dollars. This was the one hedge, the one investment that was open to almost everyone. The new home owners of this period were leveraged buyers; for many, the equity in their first home would finance the later purchase of a larger and more expensive one.

This was not an accident, but a conscious investment strategy that was openly promoted at the time. On *The Dick Cavett Show* in 1971, the contemporary Adam Smith told millions of viewers that houses are wonderful because society gives you a way to owe money for a long period. With a fixed-rate mortgage, if the rates go down, you can pay off the mortgage and get another one at the lower rate. If rates go up, the bank can't raise them. Since the mortgage rate isn't much higher than the inflation rate and since you can deduct the interest, the use of money is almost free. With higher interest rates from inflation, the money really will be free. "It's a one-way street, in your direction, one of the great free rides," he said.[11] By this reckoning, a mortgage was leverage without a downside.

It was an exaggeration, however, to call home ownership a free ride. One risk was always there: home owners could lose jobs during a recession, which most recently happened from 1990 to 1992, and lose both their home and the money already invested in it. Another risk, always real but seldom acknowledged, erupted in the oil bust of the Southwest in the 1980s, when the seemingly unthinkable happened—housing values collapsed. Similar if less dramatic price declines have been experienced intermittently in other regions; but sooner or later, the rebound always comes. These are the risks, but they are not reasons to decide against investing in a home. It may not be a sure thing, but it's the most secure, widespread, democratic, and immediately satisfying investment of all. It's not just a place to put your money but a place to raise your family. It's not just leverage; it's a place to live.

Mortgage lenders had not anticipated the inflationary bust of the early 1970s; as they sought to catch up and counter it, they started to market the adjustable-rate mortgage, or ARM. This type of mortgage permitted lenders to share their risk with the borrower, because its interest rates floated up and down with the market interest rates.

At the same time, a newly invigorated consumer movement pushed for additional home owner protections. Previously, states had set the rules for closings, and they had varied widely. In many jurisdictions the byword should have been "home buyer beware." But in 1974 Congress responded to consumer pressures with the Real Estate Settlement Procedures Act. The act set standards for disclosure that to this day define a consumer's rights in the mortgage application process. For example, a lender cannot require a home buyer to purchase title insurance from a specific company. Moreover, within three days of receiving a home mortgage application, a lender must disclose to a potential borrower, in writing, a good-faith estimate that includes points, fees, and the annual percentage rate for the loan.

The changes of the 1960s and 1970s also involved a shift in the kind of homes being bought and financed. Market forces increasingly accommodated to the reality that not everyone could afford the traditional detached, single-family house. As a result, the market offered more and more manufactured housing, condominiums, and town houses.

From 1960 to 1973, manufactured housing—largely mobile homes—rose from 8 percent to 27.6 percent of the nation's annual housing starts.[12] Soon after, however, purchases trailed off, and today only 7 percent of home owners live in such housing.[13] Similarly, throughout the 1980s condominiums accounted for 9 to 17 percent of housing starts.[14] At first, few lenders wanted to be involved with condominiums, but Fannie Mae stepped in to encourage and assist their financing. Later, the corporation did the same for cooperative housing. Condominiums and town houses are clearly here to stay: they have proved to be an important door to home ownership for singles, young couples, and senior citizens. Moreover, in expensive, high-density, high-demand areas, they have often been the only viable form of home ownership for average Americans. In a condo, the buyer receives title to a specific unit and a proportional interest in the common areas of the complex. This is different from a cooperative, or co-op, in which a corporation owns the land and buildings and the buyers are shareholders, each with the right to live in a specific unit.

As the 1970s drew to a close, the continuing innovations in housing and mortgage finance brought the home ownership rate to a historic high of over 65 percent. This represented an astounding postwar leap: the rate had risen by half since the end of the war and seemed foreordained to continue rising indefinitely. Although 1980 was marked by both inflation and an economic downturn, no one predicted that the decade ahead would witness a decline in home ownership rates for the first time in half a century.

4

A Dream in Peril?

The United States, for the first time in decades, experienced a declining home ownership rate in the 1980s and 1990s—from 65.6 percent in 1980 to 65.0 percent in 1995. This was not a single, simple trend, however, but the product of a series of complicated factors. First, the most serious inflation of the postwar period hit during the late 1970s and early 1980s. While inflation was raging, the deepest recession in decades struck. Then, ten years later, there was another severe recession that destroyed jobs and again depressed the housing market. Second, high interest rates prevailed throughout much of the 1980s; it was harder to buy a home and often hard to sell one. Third, the demographic landscape was changing profoundly. In 1950, married couples headed 79 percent of all households; by 1994 the figure was only 56 percent.[1] The number of children living with only one parent has doubled since 1970.[2] As of 1993, 80 percent of all married couples in the United States owned their own home, a figure far above the national average and far above the rate for single parents.[3] Demography, it appears, is also destiny in determining home ownership.

But the decline involved more than changing patterns of marriage and family. For example, the home ownership rate for married couples under twenty-five with children declined from 38.8 percent to 23.8 percent between 1980 and 1992, and it fell from 33.6 percent to 27.1 percent for childless couples in this age bracket. Even in a group for which it should have been rising rapidly, couples between twenty-five and thirty-four with children, home ownership fell sharply in this period, from 71.1 percent to 60.5 percent.[4]

The inflation of the late 1970s provoked interest rate increases to unheard-of levels—14 percent or more for mortgages—and this in turn made homes less affordable. In 1972 the Housing Affordability Index of the National Association of Realtors reached a high of 154.8 (at 100, a median-income family can afford to buy a median-priced home). The index collapsed to 68.9 in 1981 and did not climb even as high as 114 until 1987. Then it dropped again. Finally, in the 1990s, as interest rates fell to their lowest level in twenty years, affordability again improved; the index rose to 133.3 in 1993.

A 1991 survey examined renters aged twenty-five to thirty-four to determine how mortgage rates limited their ability to qualify for a thirty-year, fixed-rate loan. With rates at 10 percent, only 31.7 percent of these renters had enough income to buy a home. At 9 percent, the proportion of mortgage-eligible renters rose to 36.3 percent. And at an 8 percent mortgage rate, more than 40 percent could qualify for a mortgage.[5]

Interest rates are only one hurdle on the home ownership track, however. Often, young households face an even tougher challenge—finding the up-front cash for a down payment and closing costs. A 10 percent down payment on a $150,000 house, which would be difficult to find in most of suburban Washington, D.C., equals $15,000 in cold hard cash. Add to that $4,050 to pay a three-point origination fee on a $135,000 mortgage plus another $3,000 in taxes and closing costs, and the tab rises to over $22,000. Even if a young couple finds a less expensive house, a lack of up-front cash can stop them from buying.

This is a problem that compounds over time; an entire segment of this generation may never be able to move up the housing ladder. According to the 1993 report of the Joint Center for Housing Studies:

To the extent that young households delay becoming homeowners because they lack the savings to cover . . . upfront costs, they remain locked out of a primary savings and investment vehicle. This, then, is the vicious circle would-be buyers face: lack of savings and wealth prevents them from securing a home, the very asset that has proven to be the best source of wealth accumulation for the vast majority of American households. . . . [In other words, they won't be able to sell, take the profit, and move up to a better home.] With a median net wealth of only $2,096, only 25 percent of younger renter households could cover the 10 percent down payment of closing costs. . . . Among minority households only 13.6 percent have the upfront cash—less than half the share that have sufficient income to qualify for a mortgage [at an 8 percent interest rate].[6]

One barrier has persisted, despite changing laws and measurable progress, through low interest rates and high, recession and prosperity, and changes in demography. Across the decades, discrimination has denied many minority households access to a home, both as a place to live and as a major source of capital accumulation. This is a major reason why minority communities have not seen accumulated wealth flowing from generation to generation at nearly the same rate as in the white community. Each minority generation starts behind economically. The impact is measurable and profound: in 1991, the net worth of whites was nearly ten times that of blacks.[7] This cycle repeats itself, as lower net worth translates into less money available to assist the next generation when it needs help with a down payment and closing costs. Married black couples, who still find themselves behind white couples, actually increased their home ownership rate from 61.8 percent to 66.8 percent during the 1980s.[8] They were one of the few groups to do so. But they had a lot of catching up to do, and their progress came in spite of the continuing prevalence of racial discrimination.

Home ownership, as the concept was defined by the arriving colonists, has existed for nearly four centuries on this continent. From the start, home ownership has helped define the nation, first across a vast wilderness and then across a vast and diverse range of people. It became a common dream, a powerful shared aspiration, one of the common characteristics that brought and held us together as a people.

Other nations are united by the compactness of their geography, a common religion, or a common culture that stretches far back. America has been called an idea—the one nation that is primarily an idea—and among the most powerful of the American ideas is home ownership. It is a symbol and a guarantor of personal autonomy and individual property rights, and yet it also underlies our sense of community. Democracy and home ownership are two distinctive but related American visions.

Home Ownership Around the World

Perhaps because certain social forces have greater effect in other nations, home ownership rates are decidedly lower in many of the democracies of Western Europe. But some of these governments are taking steps to increase home ownership, perhaps because they now see the need to give people a greater stake in their society.

The home ownership rate here (65 percent) far outpaces that in Germany (40 percent), France (54 percent), and Austria (50 percent).[9] In Switzerland, the home ownership rate is so low (30 percent) that the government has embarked on sweeping reforms, including a law to let Swiss citizens tap their pension funds to purchase homes.

Britain

The greatest increase in home ownership of any European nation in the 1980s, and the greatest effort to achieve it, was seen in Great

Britain. This was due to a large extent to the deliberate policies of a conservative government. The home ownership rate soared from 58.6 percent to 66.4 percent—higher than in the United States. Although the average British home may be smaller than the typical American home, the Britain that was called "a nation of shop-keepers" is now a leading home-owning nation. The Thatcher government, which came to power in 1979, led the way with a far-reaching plan for the privatization of public housing. Families in "council houses," as they were known, were not only urged to buy them, they were offered terms that were difficult to refuse. Former Secretary of Housing and Urban Development Jack Kemp has argued for a similar approach in the United States.

The Thatcher government also encouraged new kinds of mort-gage flexibility for all home buyers—for example, top-up interest only and second mortgages. The consequence was not only greater home ownership but greater liquidity: people could borrow against their houses, using them as a source of investment capital.

The British government seemed to have achieved an elusive but fundamental goal—increasing the wealth of the mass of its citizens. By 1991, owner-occupied homes in Britain accounted for 40 percent of the wealth held by individuals. One observer wrote, "Greater ability to borrow against housing wealth, and more specifically to extract equity, enhances the real value of housing because owner occupied dwellings become a fungible source of wealth. Thus, part of the rise in the real value of houses in the 1980s may be due to the process of financial liberalization [and] may prove to be permanent."[10]

But that permanence was not to be. The early 1990s saw a sharp downturn in the British housing market, a falloff triggered by a poorly managed monetary policy whose effects have been as bad as the inflation it was aimed to prevent. The sharp rise in interest rates pushed housing prices down 10 to 30 percent and brought on a 50 percent decline in housing sales between 1988 and 1992. In 1993, thirty-day delinquencies on mortgage payments in Britain were running at an astounding 15 to 25 percent. The government policy of providing subsidies for unemployed home owners helped prevent a wider housing bust, but one out of every eight home owners in the country actually developed negative equity due to the downturn. By August 1994, the value of the average British home had fallen by £7,000 since 1989.[11]

The lack of a mature secondary mortgage market—a Freddie Mac or a Fannie Mae—aggravated the problem. Without large secondary mortgage institutions to set standards for the loans they will buy, the British mortgage market is rife with lax underwriting. The result is that "some lenders . . . rely on the life insurance salesmen, who act as mortgage brokers, to underwrite mortgage applications. . . . These salesmen are more interested in selling a life policy than in writing a good mortgage, because their commission is tied to the life insurance policy. . . . During the housing boom, the insurance salesmen were raising the allowable loan-to-value ratio to as high as 95 percent."[12] This makes the market even more vulnerable to downturns.

Japan

The link between home ownership and democracy is powerfully visible in Japan. As the country became democratic for the first time in its history, it also gained more home owners. At 61 percent, the Japanese home ownership rate is now almost comparable to that of the United States. The desire to own is so strong that it overcomes obstacles that would be regarded as intolerable in the United States. An average Japanese house costs 5.7 times the average family income, while the average U.S. home costs only 2.7 times the median income. And for all that extra money, Japanese home owners buy houses that are far smaller and have fewer amenities than their American counterparts. An average Japanese house has 800 square feet of living space, compared to 1,773 square feet in the United States. Homes are so expensive in

Japan that some banks offer mortgages that extend into a family's next generation.

During his 1994 visit to the United States, then Japanese prime minister Morihiro Hosokawa said that Japanese citizens should be able to buy a home at "about two-thirds the present average cost."[13] For a long time, even as home ownership has risen, the Japanese government has made this goal all but impossible by subordinating the interests of home owners and consumers to other long-term national goals. But as Japanese democracy has strengthened and one-party rule been broken, the demand for homes at a reasonable cost is slowly changing Japan's economic course.

Developing Nations

That same demand has been felt in newer and poorer democracies. Under President Nelson Mandela, home ownership has become a priority for South Africans. His housing strategy for the poor is private ownership, much like the Thatcher approach in Britain; he specifically rejects an overreliance on public housing with subsidized rents. The government will provide up to $4,300 as a capital grant to help a family buy or improve their home. Given the enormity of South Africa's housing crisis—a shortage that numbers in the millions—no one expects an instant solution. But the nation has been set firmly on a home-owning path. Ironically, the actual architect of the plan, President Mandela's friend and minister of housing, the late Joe Slovo, was a longtime leader of the Communist Party. But in a new South Africa and a new world, Slovo became an ardent apostle of private ownership for the blacks who had suffered under apartheid. I had the privilege of visiting South Africa in 1995 and observed many of that nation's tremendous housing needs firsthand. I was struck by the enormous potential for innovative public-private partnerships to meet the incredible challenges faced there. From the squatter camps of Soweto to the housing developments in the townships outside Cape Town, the South African people bring a remarkable spirit to the task of building a free and democratic nation of home owners.

Barriers to Home Ownership

Here in America, private ownership of homes by minorities will never reach a satisfactory level until we overcome the effects of racial discrimination. When he wrote that "Good fences make good neighbors," the poet Robert Frost meant the opposite.

There are reams of surveys and stacks of studies that testify to the essential truth that in many different ways, home ownership and citizenship go together. Home ownership as a value—a basic family value, if you will—is a tenet that has been sounded by American presidents from Jefferson to Roosevelt to our own day. And the more evidence we gather, the more empirical support there is for its validity.

Yet we also know more about the barriers to home ownership than ever before. Millions can't afford a home, many by a margin of only a few dollars. Others don't know how to buy one. Others face the persistent, often barely disguised roadblock of racial discrimination. This is the single greatest quantifiable barrier to minority Americans' buying their own home. It is the factor that most directly denies people the quintessential American dream—and it is also the most shameful, doing so by flouting America's own professed ideals.

5

Dismantling the Barriers
of Discrimination

In 1990, the home ownership rate for black Americans born in the United States stood at 44.5 percent, far below the nearly 70 percent rate for native-born white Americans. While some of this disparity reflects differences in household formation, black married couples also lag far behind white married couples in home ownership. In fact, the African-American home ownership rate would rise above 58 percent, a jump of one-third, if black Americans only achieved the same rate as whites of similar age, income, and family type.[1] These numbers tell a tale not simply of economic inequality but of discrimination.

That discrimination wears a variety of masks. It takes the form not only of overt acts but also of subtle patterns and offers never even made. Fair housing laws would be simple to write and enforce if the problem were straightforward. Then, perhaps, to use President Kennedy's phrase, discrimination truly could be "wiped out with the stroke of a pen." But it has not been easy to fight discrimination in housing, and some of the hardest battles are still unwon.

The civil rights movement is a proud part of our national history, and its legacy is a continuing part of our national life. It is largely with legislation passed in the 1960s that we are still combating housing discrimination, adapting the laws to the changing challenges of covert prejudice.

The seminal case concerning segregation, *Brown* v. *Board of Education of Topeka*, dealt with the public schools, not public or private housing. In 1957, three years after *Brown,* President Eisenhower was forced to send federal troops to enforce the integration of schools in Little Rock, Arkansas; a less dramatic but equally important event was the passage in New York City of the first laws prohibiting racial discrimination in housing. Other cities and states followed New York's example, but federal action on housing was slower in coming. The early civil rights acts—of 1957 and 1960—were silent on the issue. The 1964 act prohibited discrimination in employment and in public accommodations like hotels and restaurants. (The act was spurred, in part, by the lunch counter sit-ins which were emblematic of the nonviolent protests of the early 1960s.) Then came the Voting Rights Act of 1965. It followed the famous march across Alabama to the town of Selma (in which I participated) and President Lyndon Johnson's call, in a speech to Congress, to embrace the civil rights movement in national policy.

It took the assassinations of both Dr. Martin Luther King Jr. and Senator Robert Kennedy, and the riots that followed the King killing, to create enough impetus to push through the first federal open housing law. The Fair Housing Act of 1968, authored by my long-time employer, mentor, and friend, former Vice President Walter F. Mondale, made it unlawful anywhere in the United States to discriminate on the basis of race, color, sex, religion, or national origin in the selling, renting, or financing of housing. It was not until six years later, however, that the Equal Credit Opportunity Act gave fair housing laws the necessary backup, by attacking discrimination in credit, mortgage, and lending policies. The Community Reinvestment Act of 1977 added an affirmative-action obligation on the part of depositories to meet the credit needs of low- and moderate-income neighborhoods. The Home Mortgage Disclosure Act provided critical information to fight discrimination by requiring public disclosure of mortgage lending patterns.

But there was increasing resistance along with this progress. This was also the time when the expression *white backlash* was born. In 1964, President Kennedy's former press secretary, Pierre Salinger, then a senator from California, lost his seat because he defended the state's fair housing act, which was overwhelmingly repealed in a popular referendum. Alabama Governor George Wallace challenged President Johnson in several 1964 primaries and received as much as 42 percent of the vote (in Maryland). In 1966, the surprise Democratic nominee for governor of Maryland, George Mahoney, assailed open housing and ran on the slogan "A Man's Home Is His Castle." The state's civic leaders and newspapers, including the *Washington Post,* rallied to Mahoney's opponent, Spiro T. Agnew, then a liberal Republican unknown even to the voters of Maryland. Two years later he would reverse field and become vice president in a campaign that followed the "Southern Strategy" of going slowly on civil rights.

Using the powers granted by open housing laws, administrations of both parties have increasingly attacked redlining (the refusal to offer mortgage loans within a minority neighborhood), a practice that, in effect, equates race with risk. The Federal Office of Thrift Supervision has warned institutions that it is not enough to not discriminate in granting loans once they're applied for; institutions cannot engage in marketing practices or business relationships that "improperly restrict . . . clientele to segments of the community."[2] Tough enforcement of these laws and rules wins strong support from minority and community groups, but many lending institutions question the costs and necessity of so much regulatory oversight. The fact remains, however, that before such legislation was passed, scores of banks in effect hung out signs to potential home buyers that read "No Blacks or Hispanics Need Apply." Also, single and divorced women found it difficult to obtain credit—whether it was a mortgage or just a credit card.

The fair housing laws grant federal agencies a wide range of enforcement powers. In the areas of lending, they have the authority to levy fines and to force a financial institution to retrain its employees, recast its marketing strategies, revamp its internal auditing practices, and reverse policies that inhibit minority lending. Financial institutions can also be ordered to pay damages or offer loans to customers injured by discriminatory practices.[3]

The two agencies chiefly responsible for investigating cases of mortgage discrimination and enforcing the laws against it are the Justice Department and the Department of Housing and Urban Development (HUD). The Justice Department can initiate an investigation on its own, or it can respond directly to complaints or referrals from elsewhere in the federal government. The department can impose civil monetary penalties and file federal lawsuits. It has the power to order the retooling of a bank's policies or the retraining of its personnel.

HUD can investigate discrimination in response to a complaint or on its own, without receiving one. It has subpoena power, and it can authorize the Justice Department to issue temporary and preliminary injunctions. HUD can decide cases and issue fines administratively, unless one of the parties involved demands that a federal judge hear the arguments. The department also has the power to direct Fannie Mae or Freddie Mac to take remedial action against discriminatory lenders, including suspension, probation, reprimand, and settlement.

The home-buying and home-lending process is affected by other federal agencies at specific points. For example, the Federal Housing Finance Board, which has no direct enforcement powers under the fair lending laws, can take action against certain banks that receive adverse regulatory or judicial rulings. There are many forms of housing discrimination and many sources of prejudice, so it's probably natural and inevitable that the federal response has become multipronged.

But despite all the laws, efforts, and regulations, despite the very real progress that has been made, housing discrimination and segregation continue to blight countless neighborhoods and the entire national landscape. In the 1994 Fannie Mae *National Housing*

Survey, 74 percent of blacks, 63 percent of Hispanics, and 54 percent of whites said that housing discrimination in the United States was a "serious problem" or "one of the two or three most serious problems" in the country. Similar percentages saw the same problems with mortgage availability.

In the survey, African Americans regarded discrimination and other social barriers as the second greatest obstacle to buying a home—ahead of job insecurity, debt level, insufficient income, and bad credit records. Like other renters, African-American renters rate down payments and cost as their biggest worries. But half of all blacks who rent thought it would be difficult to find a neighborhood where they could feel confident of buying a home. Only 26 percent of whites who rent expressed this concern. Overall, 54 percent of African Americans in the 1994 survey believed that blacks face discrimination in the mortgage process all or most of the time. Thirty-nine percent of Hispanics thought they faced the same problem. Only 26 percent of whites agreed that blacks and Hispanics face discrimination.

Hispanics were more likely to think they could overcome social barriers. Only 17 percent of them considered discrimination a major obstacle to home buying. But African Americans were split evenly over whether blacks and other minorities have the same chance as whites to buy any type of housing they can afford. The split is a sign of how far we have to go, but is also powerful evidence of how far we have come. Thirty years ago, the vast majority of blacks would have denied that they had even remotely equal access to home ownership; fifty years ago, virtually none would have thought so.

Inner-City Housing

Two critical inner-city issues affect both the housing stock and the ability of people to own a home. Both issues disproportionately affect minorities, who are so often forced to live in the inner cities.

The first is lead paint. The number one environmental problem for children in America today is exposure to lead, and the number one vehicle for lead exposure is peeling paint in older buildings. Lead stunts children's growth and mental development. There are no symptoms.

Often, removing lead paint in a building costs substantially more than the price of the structure itself. So there is an almost irresistible incentive to abandon a structure that's about to be ticketed by the local government for a lead paint violation.

At Fannie Mae, we have attempted to respond by creating the National Center for Lead Safe Housing and funding it with $5.5 million. Because the lead in older structures can't be eradicated entirely, the center is committed to a containment strategy. The key is to find ways to seal and protect walls with lead paint on them—for example, by applying a cellophane coating so the paint can't flake off. This problem is a veritable engine of urban decay, but Fannie Mae and others have been making progress in fighting it. We still have a long struggle ahead, which must progress building by building, block by block, city by city.

One of the most attractive "new" ideas for revitalizing urban centers, at least on the surface, is private ownership of public housing. As we've seen, the idea has been tried and has succeeded in Britain. It seems like a natural transition to home ownership, especially for the black and Hispanic families already living there.

The difficulty is that as soon as people have a choice, privatized public housing is not where they want to live. Almost nobody sees public housing as a destination, a goal. Residents see it as a temporary location, a place to leave, not a place to live permanently. Many of them even see it as a place where they are captive or held prisoner. They worry about the crime there; they know about the black-market opportunities. But hardly anybody, black, Asian, Hispanic, or white, sees public housing as a desirable home.

In short, the fatal flaw of privatizing public housing is that it is not anyone's dream to live in a small apartment in an economically and racially segregated inner-city high-rise. People in public housing, especially those with the capacity to own, have the same vision as everybody else in America. They want to own a house—even if it's remote, even if it's a long commute—that has grass and some trees and is in a neighborhood where their kids can ride a bike and go to a school without fear. Moreover, even for those who prefer urban living, privatized public housing has none of the attributes of affluence associated with conventional town-house, apartment, or co-op living.

Promoting home ownership as a way of increasing people's net worth and thus giving them a stake in their community is the right course. But since public housing offers an unwanted environment, privatizing it is a policy that's ultimately unsustainable.

The policy has another and dangerous flaw. In many cases, privatizing public housing tends to perpetuate racial separation. We cannot continue to have the kind of physical racial segregation we live with today and have a healthy society, nor can we afford to accept or reinforce our nation's present economic segregation.

But we can't change this situation overnight; we need to look at a range of small-scale solutions and apply them on a neighborhood-by-neighborhood basis in both the cities and the suburbs. We have to develop private market mechanisms to give those with minimum sufficient incomes a genuine chance to break free of the racial discrimination that has been prevalent in real estate selling and finance, so that they can integrate themselves.

Millions of people in the United States are economically qualified to have a home but don't because of lack of information, fear of the system, or an inability to take advantage of job opportunities. The lack of sufficient public transportation in the United States locks many families out of home ownership because their breadwinners can't get a job in the community they want to live in. They would accept the inconvenience, but they often find that there is literally no practical way to commute. One Fannie Mae survey quantified the sacrifices people would make for home ownership: they would take a second job; they would put their children in day care; they would drive twice the distance they currently drive to work. If people are given a road map to a safe environment through home ownership, they will take it. But the road maps don't exist for millions of Americans.

The Possibilities of the Urban Housing Stock

Yet much of the inner-city housing stock represents a major untapped seedbed for home ownership. There are a number of cities that have taken advantage of their existing high-quality housing stock. Cleveland is a prime example. Cleveland hit bottom in the late 1980s. Now, because of the high quality of its housing stock, people have been reviving and rehabbing the city's neighborhoods. A housing dollar goes much further in Cleveland than in its suburbs; consequently, more and more families have been willing to take on the challenge of dealing with security and neighborhood cleanup. In St. Louis there are a large number of potentially attractive four-family units. In most cases they're too small, so they're being converted into two-unit buildings, and they're selling well.

But usually it's not enough for the housing itself to be affordable and attractive. Lending institutions—and this is something Fannie Mae is doing—have to be prepared to offer mortgages that not only provide the funds needed to purchase a home, but also help finance the cost of rehabbing the home. The availability of such mortgage credit will help these neighborhoods come back.

All this requires more, from both the private and public sectors—at the very time when we are facing a major federal withdrawal from housing policy. In 1994 HUD's overall budget was approximately $29 billion; in 1996 it will be $19 billion.

This massive downsizing of the federal role could have profound repercussions across our society. If we continue to have increasing income and race segregation, declining economic prospects for entire groups of people, and increasing home ownership costs, we may sentence this society to endemic social disintegration.

We have seen the tinderbox effect of social injustice several times in recent decades. Detroit is a warning of how civil disorder can become, in effect, a chronic, daily condition. Not only is Detroit being depopulated, but the city's structures are being torn down, leaving vast areas of vacant land that no one proposes to build on. When people see this literal hopelessness, they themselves tend to lose hope. In my view, the idea of family cohesion is closely related to home ownership. If people have a stable and safe place to live, there is a far better chance to keep a family together.

If we decide, consciously or by neglect, that our central cities are finished, it will be difficult for America to sustain a viable society. We need a strategy to prevent our cities from becoming increasingly vacant and to prevent the few who remain from becoming more and more racially and economically concentrated, more and more homogeneous. We need a strategy to stop and reverse the flight of almost anybody who can afford to leave. Otherwise, we will face a grim competition for dwindling resources between hollowed-out cities and the rest of the nation. America will become two societies, with a new social dividing line between home owners and those who are locked out, poorer, more despairing, and angrier than before, their minority status reinforced by their lack of ownership and even the potential for gaining it.

Discrimination in Lending

As of 1994, one out of five blacks and one out of six Hispanics said they had personally experienced prejudice when applying for a mortgage.[4] Discrimination is the single biggest issue we have to face in the lending community. Long after the national commitment to open housing began, the problems run the gamut from a shortage of minority employees in the mortgage and real estate industry to steering prospective home buyers away from certain areas to patently inadequate outreach.

The easiest discrimination to attack and remedy is overt discrimination—for example, if lenders have a stated policy of limiting maximum loan amounts for people under thirty years old or openly acknowledge that they "prefer not to grant mortgages to blacks and Hispanics." This, obviously, is not the heart of the problem; it is flagrant, patently stupid, as well as wrong and illegal.

There is a second kind of discrimination, however: disparate treatment. This kind of discrimination can be directly proved, even though it does not include overt denial of minority applicants. A lender says, in effect, "Of course we loan to everyone," but then makes the actual application process more difficult for minority applicants. As a federal task force reported in 1994, "Disparate treatment . . . does not require any showing that the treatment was motivated by prejudice or a conscious intention to discriminate against a person beyond the difference in the treatment itself. It is considered by courts to be intentional discrimination because no credible, nondiscriminatory reason explains the difference in treatment on a prohibited basis."[5] For example, an institution violates the law if it takes loan information and determines qualifications quickly and with no fee from a white applicant but requires fees from minority applicants and forces them to wait for a decision.

More difficult for the law and the courts are cases where the primary evidence of discrimination involves results, not intentions. This is called disparate impact; it occurs when a lender's policies or practices appear to treat all applicants equally, but the outcomes disproportionately disadvantage a particular group. Individuals of one race, sex, or age are approved less often, even though they are similar in characteristics such as economic circumstances. If a lender uses the policies at issue for a justifiable "business necessity" and there are no available nondiscriminatory alternatives, then the institution has not violated the law.

The system attempts to cover the full range of discrimination, which is limited only by the ingenuity of loan officers or real estate agents determined to get around the law. But between the law and life there is an inevitable gap. How wide is it? How prevalent is mortgage discrimination, in all its various forms? The most comprehensive research comes from Boston; it was stimulated when data required under the Federal Home Mortgage Disclosure Act showed much higher mortgage denial rates there for African-American and Hispanic applicants than for whites. Not only were minorities there two to three times as likely as whites to have their loans denied, but high-income minorities were turned down more often than low-income white applicants.

Common sense would see this as clear-cut proof of discrimination. But before reaching that conclusion, there are underlying questions, such as the applicants' financial resources, records, and liabilities, that have to be examined and weighed to see if race and race alone was the decisive factor. This is precisely what the Federal Reserve Bank of Boston did, releasing its findings in October 1992 in a document that has already become a classic study of mortgage discrimination.[6]

On the basis of race alone, minority applicants were denied mortgages at a rate 2.7 times higher than that of whites. Then the Boston Fed surveyed nonracial factors and reported that "minority applicants, on average, do have greater debt burdens, higher loan-to-value ratios and weaker credit histories and they are less likely to buy single-family homes than white applicants, and . . . these disadvantages do account for a large portion of the difference in denial rates." But even then, after rigorously eliminating all nonracial factors that could conceivably have influenced the decision, minorities were still 1.6 times more likely to be denied mortgages than whites. This is true, the Boston Fed emphasizes, "even after controlling for financial, employment, and neighborhood characteristics." In the Boston metropolitan area, there is a 17 percent mortgage denial rate for minorities, compared to an 11 percent denial rate for whites with the same financial and property attributes. The Federal Reserve study cited this as "a statistically significant gap . . . associated with race."[7] It is an undeniable reality, irrefutable proof of the continuing distance between our professed principles as a nation and the often shameful practices of our institutions.

The mortgage application process is subject to the effects of prejudice because, for all its forms and standards, it is not completely mechanical. It is not the financial equivalent of turning a key in a car ignition—if the key fits, the engine starts. Automobiles don't know the skin color of the driver. At stage after stage of the mortgage application process, human discretion intrudes—and, naturally, so does discrimination.

In the first stage of the process, a prospective home buyer fills out a standard application, at the lender's office, by mail, by telephone, or during a home visit from a lender or mortgage broker. Right off the bat, a loan officer can decide whether an applicant is likely to be approved. The Boston Fed study describes what is right—and potentially wrong—with this: "If the loan does not appear viable, the lender may make its credit decision at that time and deny the application. The initial review process saves some borrowers application fees, but also represents the first level of discretion in the process."[8] In short, if you're white, you've saved the money it would have cost to go further. But if you're black or Hispanic, you have to wonder about the real reason you were turned down.

If a prospective buyer passes this initial screen, the lender next verifies the information on the application and orders an appraisal that values the property's worth. As the numbers are evaluated, subjectivity once again enters the process.[9] On the surface, the process doesn't look subjective—in theory, all that's really happening is "crunching the numbers." To ensure that a loan can be sold on the secondary market, the lender will apply certain formulas established by Fannie Mae and Freddie Mac, the largest buyers in that market. In general, borrowers should not be spending more than 28 percent of their household income on housing costs. For example, if a husband and wife together earn $50,000 a year, they can afford to pay $1,166 a month toward their housing expenses, including mortgage principal and interest payments, property taxes, and home owner's insurance. A mortgage for them should be approved if the fully amortized, comprehensive monthly payment is lower than $1,166 and the couple has an unblemished credit history and no extraordinary debt that pushes their total monthly obligations (which can also include debts such as student loans and car loans) beyond 36 percent of monthly income.

What could be more mechanical? In fact, there are elements of discretion. In the real world, the vast majority of borrowers don't possess perfect records and the precise debt and income ratios to meet the required standards. The Boston Fed study found that "less than 20 percent of borrowers [white or minority] are without blemish and, therefore, lenders are left considerable room for subjectivity and discretion."[10] Among the "compensating factors" that can improve a loan application to the levels necessary to sell the mortgage on the secondary market are favorable letters from creditors, calculations of future earning potential, or a significant down payment. Flexibility is built into the process.

If applicants clearly meet or exceed the Fannie Mae and Freddie Mac standards, they are in fact almost certain to be approved. Well-heeled, well-qualified minorities are not turned down because of the color of their skin. In the Boston Fed study, 97 percent of minorities with unblemished credentials were approved. But applicants who fall into that category, white or black, are themselves a distinct minority: "The majority of borrowers—both white and minority—are not perfect, and lenders have considerable discretion over the extent to which they consider these imperfections as well as compensating factors."[11] In that consideration lies the possibility for discrimination, making Hispanics and blacks 60 percent more likely to be rejected.

Some critics contend that the Boston study is flawed. They claim that if white applicants are receiving preferential treatment, then the default rate of white borrowers should exceed that of African-American borrowers, which in fact it doesn't. But when the Fannie Mae Office of Housing Research reviewed the Boston Fed's study, it found that after correcting "miscoded or atypical observations," an analysis based on entirely clean data confirmed the effects of race: "In fact, a closer examination of the data reveals an even stronger case of discrimination in the Boston market than was revealed by the original report."[12]

Discrimination also motivates and results from redlining. In effect, a line is drawn around certain neighborhoods, and banks and other lenders avoid marketing there. The law puts the burden of proof on financial institutions to demonstrate that their marketing is nondiscriminatory. The law is often violated, however. The *Atlanta Journal and Constitution* won the 1989 Pulitzer Prize for a series on redlining in the Atlanta area. The series reported that banks and S&Ls favored white areas by a margin of five to one and that "race—not home value or household income—consistently determines the lending patterns of metro Atlanta's largest financial institutions." One article described a distinct relationship between race and mortgage loans: "Among stable neighborhoods of the same income, white neighborhoods always received the most bank loans per 1,000 single-family homes. Integrated neighborhoods always received fewer. Black neighborhoods—including the mayor's neighborhood—always received the fewest."[13]

The series did point to a positive development: black-owned banks in Atlanta seemed to be capitalizing on the failure of larger institutions to serve minority clients and neighborhoods. One black-owned bank, which loans almost exclusively in black neighborhoods in the Atlanta metropolitan area, has experienced the lowest default rate on real estate loans of any bank of its size in the United States.[14] Of course, African Americans can't rely solely on black-owned lending institutions; there aren't enough of them. So the Justice Department has moved against other banks. In a 1994 settlement with the department, Decatur Federal Savings and Loan, based in suburban Atlanta, agreed to open a branch in a primarily African-American area of the city.

Redlining is not just a southern problem—it is nationwide. The year before the Atlanta study, the *Detroit Free Press* found that those living in white neighborhoods in the Detroit metropolitan area received mortgage loans at three times the rate of those living in black neighborhoods who had similar characteristics. The newspaper cited the lack of blacks on the board of Detroit's banks as one cause for the disparity. Morris Hood, a black state legislator, attacked the banks: "The American Dream is to own a home, to own a business. Blacks in Detroit are being excluded from that dream."[15]

As they struggled to achieve it anyway, the area's African Americans, frustrated as they sought home loans from banks, were forced to rely increasingly on mortgage firms. Such firms made only half the mortgage loans in white areas but 70 percent of loans in 25 similar black areas. Banks assailed the methodology of the *Free Press*'s series, but Michigan's banking commissioner reported that the newspaper's findings were "consistent with trends we have observed in our yearly report on mortgage lending in Michigan." He explained, "We believe that mortgage demand may be heavily influenced by marketing and that discriminatory marketing patterns and credit steering may provide a foundation for patterns of disinvestment."[16]

Other studies in other cities reveal similar patterns.

A 1992 *Newsday* analysis of mortgage applications to New York City lenders found that blacks were 1.4 times as likely as whites to be turned down for a mortgage. Hispanics were denied 1.2 times as often as whites, while Asians were rejected at approximately the same rate as white applicants. *Newsday* cautioned that the data "cannot prove by itself that a lender discriminates. The data does not include any details about the borrower's credit and employment history—factors that may legitimately cause a lender to turn down a loan application.[17] But the clear inference is that New York City, the first jurisdiction to pass a fair housing law, still suffers from home-lending discrimination. Even if all other factors were removed, it's difficult to doubt that race matters here, as it apparently does wherever the issue is examined.

A 1993 *Washington Post* series was directly responsible for a federal investigation into discriminatory lending practices. The Justice
Department launched an investigation of the Chevy Chase Federal
Savings Bank after a *Post* story reported that only 14 of the 956
mortgage loans the bank made in 1991 were in predominantly black
neighborhoods. Chevy Chase and its mortgage subsidiary, B. F. Saul,
denied charges of redlining, but settled the case by pledging to spend
$4 million to advertise and open offices in African-American areas
and another $7 million to subsidize mortgage loans for people resid-
ing in African-American areas of Washington, D.C., and Prince
Georges County, Maryland. The bank also agreed to implement staff
changes, to work more closely with black real estate brokers, and to
seek and move measurably toward achieving a market share in
African-American areas equal to its share in white neighborhoods.
Community groups hailed the settlement, but some banking experts
questioned whether it was proper for the federal government to tell
companies where to market their services.[18] That, however, is the
clear meaning and mandate of the nation's fair housing and fair
credit laws.

Discrimination by Real Estate Agents

The problem isn't just discrimination in mortgage marketing and
approvals; it also involves a number of discriminatory tactics and
techniques in marketing and selling specific houses and neighborhoods. This can start in the initial encounter between a minority customer and a real estate agent. The relationship between
an agent and any would-be buyer is never entirely direct; there
are always code words and signals to be read. Despite the increasing role of buyer's agents, most real estate agents still act on the
seller's behalf. Within this tangled web, it can be hard to read
motives or search out the maneuvers that reflect or reinforce
prejudice. Nonetheless, there are clear and quantifiable patterns of
discrimination.

In 1991, HUD released a comprehensive survey of 3,800 fair housing audits in twenty-five metropolitan areas.[19] For this study, prepared by the Urban Institute, both black and Hispanic auditors and white auditors were sent to sales and rental agents to inquire about the availability of property advertised in a major metropolitan newspaper. Minority and white customers that were identical in important household characteristics, including sufficient income to qualify for a given property, went separately to the same landlords and real estate brokers. They then independently recorded their experiences.

In some cases there was complete denial of access for minority customers; 8 percent of blacks and Hispanics couldn't even make an appointment with a sales agent or were told a house was unavailable—at the same time it was being shown to the white auditors. While complete denial affected one in twelve potential home buyers, more subtle discrimination was far more common. African-American home buyers were shown 21 percent fewer homes, and Hispanics 22 percent fewer, than their white counterparts. Forty-six percent of black auditors also rated the real estate agents' sales efforts as indifferent or hostile.

The auditors uncovered widespread "steering" as well, in which agents recommend or offer to show minority buyers homes in predominantly minority areas and avoid showing them homes in white neighborhoods. Twenty-one percent of the time, a black or Hispanic home buyer was steered into a different neighborhood than a prospective white buyer with otherwise similar characteristics and qualifications. (Steering is the mirror image of "blockbusting," in which there is a conscious strategy to change the racial composition of a neighborhood almost overnight, driving out white residents and lowering property values in a wave of panic selling. Profiteers then buy up the vacated properties at artificially low prices and sell them to minorities for a fat profit.) When all the results were added up, the Urban Institute reported to HUD that 59 percent of African Americans and 56 percent of Hispanics experience some form of discrimination when attempting to buy a home.

This study quantified discrimination; others have conveyed the problem in more human terms, sharing the real-life experiences of those who have felt discrimination. Two authors have collected stories of discrimination from the black middle class that range from personal slights to outright illegality.[20] And these stories are only the tip of the iceberg. Too rarely do African Americans turn to fair housing laws or ask for specific government intervention; this may reflect a feeling of futility in the face of prejudice or a deep-seated skepticism that the law actually means what it says or the government will really enforce it.

One black woman, a university administrator, described how she worked two jobs to afford a home. When she was ready to buy and phoned a real estate office, the white agent on the other end of the phone told her that she would like a particular neighborhood because there were no black people there. The university administrator replied: "Well, my dear, you're in for a big surprise, because if I buy it there will be a black there then—I am a black." The real estate broker just gasped and hung up the phone.[21]

The director of a Midwestern drug abuse program recounted his experience with steering: "We saw [a house] in the newspaper, called the real estate agent up and told her we wanted to look at this house. We got out of the car and we could see the lady sitting at the table, the owner of the home, as we got out of the car in the driveway. And I actually saw the expression on her face change as she saw this young black couple walking up the driveway. I guess she figured we couldn't afford a house, or else she didn't want to give us one in this neighborhood. . . . After [the agent] got through showing us this house she drove all the way to the other side into Stonebridge Heights [which is 99 percent black] to show us another house."

He eventually bought a home around the block from the original house he looked at, in a neighborhood where he and his family are the only African Americans. "The other thing that made me realize that it was discrimination," he said, "is how many of you have ever seen a real estate agent who has never called back a prospective buyer? This woman *never* called us back, and never wanted to know if we were still looking or interested."[22]

A black real estate broker has seen the same reality from the other side of the transaction:

> There have been times when I used to sell real estate that I know that the other [agent] will not want to give me a key to show the house because he thinks that the client that I'm showing the house to is black. And that happened about four years ago, where the house was in a white executive area. The other broker thought that my clients were black, but as it turned out, both my clients were white, and more than that, my client's father knew the broker. And when they discovered what was happening, that I wasn't getting the key so they could see the house, they wanted to buy this house, she just stopped. She said, "Stop right here at this phone booth in the middle of the street." She called her father. Her father called him. And immediately when I went back to the office, the key was available. That's the way it works. . . . It was all based on their belief that I had a black client.[23]

A financial analyst at a Fortune 500 company described his own blunt response to steering: "I hired a realtor to show me around," he said, "and I gave her the requirements I was looking for—the price range, the type of house, and so forth. And, at one point in time, she steered me toward a certain section of town which made me feel a little uneasy. And, henceforth, I had a new realtor."[24] Too many minority shoppers don't take that option, or they doubt they would find anyone better. They don't accept the discrimination, but they expect it. They know what happens. As the director of one urban think tank explained, "An agent will rely on code words, telling a white person, 'You wouldn't feel comfortable here,' while a black person will be told, 'There's nothing in your price range here.' Frequently steering behavior consists of showing a black potential home buyer a house priced at $150,000 after they've told the realtor to look for a house for no more than $125,000. It's about the persistent feeling of being unwelcome. It's about racism with a smile."[25]

Minority home buyers facing subtle forms of discrimination can pursue legal remedies under the Fair Housing Act, but a lawsuit is rarely the easiest option for anyone. A lawsuit is a costly and time-consuming endeavor. It requires enormous perseverance on the part of the plaintiff to bring it to completion. Rather than undertake a lawsuit, some families may conduct their home search without a real estate agent. That aside, the undeniable truth is that, in terms of social morality as well as the law, families of any race should be able to use a real estate agent without running the risk of encountering discrimination. Choosing a home—which is, in the end, so individual and human a decision—cannot be an automated or dehumanized process, and it shouldn't have to be. The code of ethics of the National Association of Realtors clearly forbids discrimination or participation in "any plan or agreement" to discriminate. The association has also negotiated a "voluntary affirmative marketing agreement" with HUD, under which members are supposed to adopt specific office procedures and work with community groups to prevent any denial of equal service. The code and the agreement almost certainly make some difference, but it would be foolish to ignore the fact that we are dealing here not just with a housing problem but with a fundamental flaw woven through the history and fabric of America.

The Road Ahead

When I was a young man in graduate school, nearly three decades ago, I worked as a consultant to the Kerner Commission, appointed by the president to identify and recommend action on the underlying causes of the devastating summer riots of 1967. That commission's fundamental finding, controversial at the time, has since become a classic statement of America's race problem: the commission found that, despite our national commitment to end discrimination, America was in danger of permanently becoming "two societies, one black, one white—separate and unequal," divided by race.[26] Twenty years later, University of Chicago professor Gary Orfield—a classmate of mine from the University of Minnesota—traced much of the nation's continuing inequality to housing segregation. It is perhaps the one effect of racial injustice that does more than any other to perpetuate and reinforce that injustice. As Professor Orfield writes, "Housing segregation is so serious because it is at the root of many other forms of segregation and inequality. It is increasingly linked to denial of opportunity for work, and it is the basis for the development of separate societies as feared by the Kerner Commission."[27]

The need for action is clear, and demands for it are rising. Old patterns of prejudice do not yield easily, voluntarily, or all at once— that much is certain after the years of trying and, yes, of real and measurable success. But that success depends on judicial and regulatory enforcement. As such enforcement has intensified in recent years, so has resistance against it. Much of the reaction against fair housing laws has consisted of explicitly non-race-based objections. Current fair housing laws and regulations are assailed as ambiguous and litigation-oriented. Using a Nexus database search, *Fortune* magazine found 1,756 news stories where the word *suit* or *lawsuit* appears within thirty words of *fair housing. Fortune*'s Daniel Seligman wrote, "The 1988 amendments, which expanded coverage to bar bias against the disabled and folks with kids, place a far greater emphasis on trials in which discriminators get nailed. . . . This brings us to the main reason fair housing is so litigation prone: Nobody knows exactly what is required. . . . The regulations are wonderfully precise about such matters as the proper dimensions of equal housing opportunity logotypes in space ads of various sizes, but hopelessly vague about which kinds of wording are discriminatory."[28]

It was Justice Oliver Wendell Holmes Jr. who observed that "hard cases make bad law." It is equally true that intractable problems demand tough action, and this fact sometimes creates complications or excesses. But any excesses that arise from enforcing fair housing pale in comparison to the evils of entrenched segregation and discrimination. Doing too much on occasion is far less damaging than doing nothing. In fact, the era of fair housing legislation has also been a time of unprecedented growth in minority home ownership. According to the Joint Center for Housing Studies of Harvard University, the home ownership rate for native-born young black American households increased from 31 percent to almost 44 percent between 1980 and 1990. For native-born young Hispanic households, the rate increased from 38 to 52 percent.[29] During the 1980s, an impressive 3.6 million Hispanics moved into the suburbs, and most of them bought homes.[30]

Immigrants who arrived in the United States during the 1970s have had a similar experience. From 1980 to 1990, the home ownership rate rose from 24 to 55 percent among young immigrant households. The increase was greatest for Asian Americans, but Mexican, Cuban, and Central American immigrants also made significant gains. In fact, the home ownership rate among those who came to the United States from Asia before 1970 already exceeds that of native-born white Americans. Seventy-five percent of them own their homes; the home ownership rate for native-born white Americans is 69 percent.

Under the umbrella of a fair housing ethic and fair housing laws, the black middle class has migrated to the suburbs in record numbers. This may be the most underreported housing story of the past twenty years. This started in the 1970s, which saw more and more black families moving out of the cities and buying homes in the suburbs. For the first time, the black population in the suburbs actually increased at a faster rate than the white population. In the 1970s, the number of African Americans in the suburbs grew by 46 percent, compared to a growth in the cities of little more than 5 percent. The trend continued into the next decade: the number of blacks living in the suburbs soared to eight million, a 34 percent increase, nearly four times greater than the rate of increase for whites. The marketing firm Claritas reported that "Black middle-class families continued to move into predominantly white suburban neighborhoods. The population of blacks in some overwhelmingly white upscale clusters more than doubled in 1990 from 1980."[31]

The 1980s were especially good for black married couples. The home ownership rate for them rose from slightly below 62 percent in 1981 to almost 67 percent in 1991. Home ownership grew much faster for black married families than for married couples as a whole, for whom the rate increased only 1 percent.

This nation has made important progress toward racial justice, but as events constantly reaffirm, we still have "miles to go before we sleep." In *The Rage of a Privileged Class*, author Ellis Close describes how even successful African Americans feel angry. Here is a typical example:

> A black director of a large bank told me of a board meeting he attended at which evidence was presented that the bank was not treating its black customers the same way it treated whites. Blacks with equivalent earnings and credit histories had significantly lower loan approval rates. The directors recognized immediately that they had a problem, that it was clear they had to do a much better job with "affirmative action." One board member bluntly disagreed, pointing out that the problem had nothing to do with affirmative action, that the bank was simply not acting in its own best interest in rejecting loans that should be approved. The black director was grateful for his colleague's intervention, for he had often seen such statements go unchallenged. The first inclination of some of his fellow board members was to consider initiatives that might benefit blacks as something other

than normal business, something that belonged in the category of charity and good works. Thus, the directors could give themselves special credit for doing what was right by any standard.[32]

Often, affirmative action seeks for minorities nothing more than what should be theirs by right. Fair housing demands only that a significant portion of society no longer be denied the same access to credit and real estate services as is enjoyed by the rest of society. The fulfillment of our democratic vision requires open and integrated communities. Halfway through the 1990s, we still have to strive for an America where no one will be discriminated against when applying for a mortgage or buying a home.

6

A Strategy for Increasing
Home Ownership in America

As we've seen, home ownership has been a defining goal of those who have come to this land from the earliest days of European settlement. It is a deeply rooted ideal, an aspiration shared today by most Americans. The dream of home ownership transcends racial and economic boundaries; it combines two of the most enduring elements of our national identity—the yearning for independence and self-determination and the bonds of community and shared responsibility.

From the ratification in 1791 of the Bill of Rights, with its guarantees of property rights, to the growth of the secondary mortgage market in our century, the course of events seems to have flowed steadily toward the expansion of home ownership. Even during periods of rapid population growth, the home ownership rate has increased, to 65 percent today.

The United States is largely a nation of home owners. But despite remarkable progress, today millions of Americans, people with steady, well-paying jobs, aspire to buy a home but have not been able to do so. Some of them are minorities who face subtle and overt discrimination; others are young people who have incomes sufficient to pay a mortgage but don't have the savings they need to cover down payments and closing costs; still others don't have enough information about the home-buying process or feel so intimidated and confused by mortgage finances that they can't successfully navigate the system or even find out if they qualify to buy a home.

It is time for a new and comprehensive strategy to break down the barriers that prevent too many American families from buying a home, even when they have the income to do so. It is time for a new strategy of home ownership, with a focus on private sector solutions. Many of the recommendations I will make here are based on initiatives pioneered at Fannie Mae, the company I lead, or at other private sector financing institutions. All of them, however, also recognize the role of the public sector and the nonprofit community.

We've already seen how the federal government's response to the housing crisis of the Great Depression led to the most dramatic rise in home ownership in American history. The Federal Housing Administration, the Veteran's Administration, and the Farmer's Home Administration have a spectacular record: because of them, over forty million families have achieved home ownership, which otherwise would have been beyond their reach.[1] Federal tax incentives for home ownership, like the deductibility of mortgage interest and property taxes, make home ownership possible and affordable for millions more. We have to emphasize private efforts, but we also have to recognize the proper role of the public sector.

Fannie Mae and Freddie Mac are prime examples of a private-public partnership. Since 1968, when Fannie Mae made the transition from a government agency to a privately managed, shareholder-owned company, it has leveraged over $1.7 trillion for investment in housing, in effect financing homes for more than twenty-five million families. The secondary market provides a foundation of stability and liquidity in mortgage financing, a source of innovation and efficiency, and a means of lowering interest rates and tapping new sources of capital for housing.

Now we must build upon the transformation, already achieved, of the housing system from a depositor-based to an investor-based system. We have seen the growth of the secondary mortgage market, the availability of more affordable options for first-time buyers, an incredible acceleration of technology, and a renewed emphasis on fighting discrimination. The strategy I offer is designed to build on these developments, to use them as leverage to produce the maximum number of new home owners. If we do that, we can see a major new increase in home ownership as early as the year 2000. By then, between 68 and 70 percent of all American families can own their own home—if we make this a priority and take a series of specific steps that are as practical as they are imperative. Our progress must be measured as it is made—in the context of a demographic revolution.

The 1990s mark the beginning of a third distinct era in American housing since World War II. Professor James W. Hughes of Rutgers University has described the three eras:

> The first era emerged in the immediate postwar years and lasted through about 1970. It was launched and sustained by the "post–World War II nesting generation" or suburbanites who were dubbed the "original Levittowners." Producing and rearing the baby boom dominated America's shelter requirements. This created a vast, homogenous, mass market.
>
> The second era, "baby boom housing demand," was driven by the direct entry of the baby boomers into the housing market. This era, which began about 1970 and lasted through the latter portions of the 1980s, redefined shelter in America. Market segmentation dynamited the previous mass market.
>
> The third era, "maturing housing demand," is powered by the demographics of aging and defines the balance of the 20th century. Households in the family-raising stage, now producing the "baby boom echo," are demanding appropriate shelter; a huge web of trade-up markets should emerge. But the bottom of the American housing market pyramid is shrinking for the first time, challenging the tradition of the move-up market.[2]

The third era will be even more revolutionary because of a development Professor Hughes could not have predicted: he did not anticipate that the 1990s would be a decade of rapid population growth fueled by increased immigration. His oversight is understandable. Virtually no one foresaw the trend. The Census Bureau's 1989 population projections have already been revised twice, in 1992 and 1993. The projected increase in U.S. population during this decade rose dramatically, from 17.8 million to 26.9 million. Much of the unanticipated increase has resulted from the Immigration Act of 1990; the 1990s will see a peak level of immigration not equaled since the first ten years of this century. And not since the "baby boom" has the overall population grown as much as it will in the 1990s.

This new demographic revolution involves more than numbers. We are in the midst of a revolution of diversity. By the year 2000, more than one in four Americans—28.4 percent—will come from a minority group. Minorities will head a quarter of all households; and among households headed by a person aged twenty-five to thirty-four, almost a third will be minorities.[3]

All of this reflects an accelerating trend. In the 1980s, the African-American population grew by 12 percent, the Asian-American population more than doubled, and the number of Hispanics in the United States rose by more than 50 percent. At the same time, the number of non-Hispanic whites increased at a rate of only 4 percent.[4] As we look to and beyond the year 2000, the trend will be most dramatic in the youngest generation of Americans. By the year 2010, the majority of children in the United States under the age of five will be minorities.[5] The diversity will reach beyond ethnic and racial composition. In the year 2000, nearly one in ten households will be headed by a single parent.[6] Almost half of the labor force will be female;[7] native-born white males will represent only 14 percent of new entrants in the labor market.[8] The population will be growing older, with more Americans in the peak home-buying years, as the number of Americans over thirty-five years old increases by twenty-six million between 1990 and 2000.[9] In 1999, every member of the baby boom generation will be over thirty-five. At the beginning of the next century, the national median age will be 35.5 years, up from 32.9 in 1990 and 29.5 in 1960.[10] In short, there will be many more potential home buyers.

But we also face a potential mismatch—between this demographic bulge and the current barriers to affordability. Two economists from the Wharton School at the University of Pennsylvania have examined the costs of home ownership over time by comparing the ability of a household of similar economic circumstances in 1960, 1974, and 1989 to buy a home of similar quality. They found that affordability remained constant between 1960 and 1974 but began to decline in the mid 1970s, when real wages for less-skilled labor failed to keep pace with home prices. Between 1974 and 1989, high school–educated workers experienced a 14.7 percent decline in real wages, which means that their real income in 1989 was only 4.1 percent higher than in 1960.[11]

There was a slight improvement in the early 1990s, when falling interest rates put home ownership within reach for millions of additional families. By 1993, affordability was at its best level since 1974. Yet the home ownership rate did not increase significantly, and by the end of 1994, affordability was falling again, as the Federal Reserve raised interest rates to head off inflation.[12]

The Wharton study also identifies trends that contribute to the decline in the capacity of families with modest income to buy a modestly priced home. The first is the correlation between a person's level of education and his or her likelihood of becoming a home owner. The study found that from 1960 to 1989, ownership was "increasingly associated with high educational attainment." In 1960, fifty percent of home owners in the study had less than a high school education, and only one in four had attended college. By 1989, the distribution was reversed. Fifty percent of home owners in 1989 had attended college. The data suggest that "single-family ownership has rapidly become only a dream for those who do not at least attend college, and this change poses a new major issue for U.S. housing policy."[13]

The second long-term trend relates to America's urban cores. The rate of home ownership in our central cities has declined dramatically. The Wharton study reports that "the American dream home was easily found—and chosen—in the cores of metropolitan areas in 1960, with just 50 percent of our sample [of home owners] located in the central city. By 1974, this proportion had fallen to one-third, and declined further to only 26 percent by 1989."[14] In large part this decline reflects a greater preference for living in suburban communities; in fact, almost all new single-family housing construction since 1974 has been located in the suburbs. But ironically, the drop-off in demand for urban housing did not bring about lower prices. By 1989, single-family homes in central cities were more costly in real dollars than they were in 1960.

A New Strategy

A dramatic decline in central-city home ownership; a drop in the number of home owners who have not attended college; profound structural, economic, and technological changes; a demographic revolution: the home ownership market is different than it was, and the differences will grow. We need a *new* American strategy for home ownership, a transformation of policy and practice as big and bold as those of the depression and postwar years. Only with a new strategy can we harness the power of the market to overcome the obstacles that stand between American families of modest means and their dream of one day becoming home owners. This strategy has ten elements.

1. Give Renters More Information

It seems simple, but it's a good place to start. All some people need to make the transition from renter to home owner is understandable, reliable information. Fannie Mae's 1994 National Housing Survey found that fewer than half of all adults have enough information to buy a home. This is particularly true for African Americans, Hispanics, people aged twenty-five to thirty-four, and people earning between $20,000 and $35,000 a year[15]—precisely the people who have the greatest problems affording a house. Also, the potential home buyers most in need of information about the process are most likely to live in central cities and less likely to have a college education.

When we set our minds to the task, this nation is superb at educating people about almost anything—from drug abuse to the importance of literacy and the threat of AIDS. We need a national consumer education campaign about home ownership opportunities for renters. It could open doors for millions. It should focus as well on fair housing and fair lending laws, to combat the discrimination that is the greatest barrier of all for many minorities.

A national consumer education campaign has to be waged on many fronts:

- *Widespread consumer advertising on television and radio.* Market research can identify the programs most watched by renters. We have to target those programs and communicate the message that there is a reliable source of information to help people explore their opportunities for home ownership. We have to offer them the necessary information to move through the home-buying process with a sense of confidence.

- *Direct mail to renters who are potential home owners.* We have to reinforce the message received from television and radio—and we have to put it in writing.

- *Home buyer fairs.* We should provide consumers with a chance to seek out information, ask questions, get advice from housing experts, meet with lenders and real estate agents, and find out exactly what they have to do to buy a home.

- *A national center for home buyer education.* This would provide a network of counselors to assist potential home buyers on a continuing basis as they work their way through the process of qualifying for a mortgage.

- *Consumer education materials.* These should be easy to understand (comprehensible not technical), reliable, and accessible at the same time.

Fannie Mae has already launched a national outreach effort of this kind.[16] We're learning from it, and we hope the lessons we take from it will help the entire industry reach out to prospective home buyers. The Fannie Mae Foundation, a nonprofit organization dedicated to expanding home ownership opportunities, which I chair, is advertising on television and radio, in print, in local markets, and to a national audience. The advertising targets young families, minorities, new immigrants, unmarried individuals, and single-parent families, the non–home owners who want to buy a home and most need to know how to do it. In 1995, we had one million responses to our advertising.

The Fannie Mae Foundation is also reaching out with direct mail. Here, too, we're targeting the groups that our surveys indicate are most uncomfortable with the home-buying process. Over the next five years, we will send tens of millions of pieces of mail to consumers, offering them the information they need to get started on a path to home ownership. We invite them to call our toll-free number, (800) 688-HOME, or return a postage-paid response card. Then, we send all who respond a copy of the consumer guide *Opening the Door to a Home of Your Own.* This guide moves step-by-step through the process of obtaining a mortgage. It includes tables to help people calculate just how much they can afford for a monthly payment. The guide is available in English, Spanish, Chinese, Korean, Vietnamese, Russian, and Haitian Creole. It's also available in braille and in video and audio versions.

The Fannie Mae Foundation's outreach campaign has its roots in the lessons we learned from a 1993 Hart-Teeter survey, which found that inequality in home ownership is closely linked with lack of information, lack of familiarity with financial transactions, lack of success in using the banking system, and lack of credit history. We learned that it's not enough simply to provide a system that embraces minorities and immigrants equally; a lot more is required for minorities and immigrants to cross the threshold. This realization inspired our information campaign, our focus on counseling, and our commitment to making sophisticated financial information available in a range of languages for potential home buyers who are not fluent in English.

Through our survey research, we've also identified a number of unusual demographic targets. For example, basketball fans—people who support local NBA teams, attend games, and watch them on television—are more likely to be renters than home owners. They make up a distinct group of people who need to hear about opportunities for home ownership. To reach them, we've formed an outreach partnership with several National Basketball Association teams. The Fannie Mae Foundation is now a sponsor of eleven NBA teams—the Atlanta Hawks, Boston Celtics, Charlotte Hornets, Cleveland Cavaliers, Golden State Warriors, Houston Rockets, Milwaukee Bucks, Portland Trailblazers, San Antonio Spurs, Seattle Supersonics, and Washington Bullets—and we air consumer advertising on game broadcasts. We encourage fans to call our toll-free number and learn more about buying a home. We send them information not only about how to apply for a mortgage but also about whether home ownership is right for them.

The Fannie Mae Foundation and team members also work together to educate basketball fans and the local community about home ownership. We jointly sponsor home-buying fairs, where team members are on hand to help bring people in. For example, in March 1996, the Washington Bullets and the Fannie Mae Foundation cosponsored a home-buying fair that drew more than seven thousand men and women, all of them ready to learn how they could become home owners.

Fannie Mae is forming other partnerships with city governments, community activists, nonprofit organizations, and mortgage lenders. We have opened twenty-five new Partnership Offices around the country to tailor our low- and moderate-income lending programs to the unique character of each community.

The most important thing we've learned is that outreach works. In just three years, 1.6 million consumers have responded to our advertising by requesting our public service consumer guides; survey research indicates that almost one in every three of these respondents goes on to buy a home within one year. We've learned as well that millions of people are confused and confounded by a mortgage process that too often seems remote and hypertechnical, but they will respond if they're offered an invitation and a map to the front door of their new home. We need a national consumer information crusade—one supported by every public and private participant in the housing finance system. I believe the results would be remarkable.

2. Discrimination in Lending

Despite all the laws and efforts directed against discrimination in housing, whites have a home ownership rate more than twenty points higher than that of blacks and Hispanics.[17] Much discrimination has been attacked, and some has been eliminated. But the home ownership gap between whites and blacks remains. And this gap makes it harder in general to bridge the economic gulf between the races: "Since homeownership is the single most prevalent and important means of wealth accumulation among American households, reduction of homeownership possibilities for blacks, Hispanics, Asians or other minorities because of such discrimination may unjustly contribute to the lower wealth status of such households as a group compared with white households."[18]

It is clear that outlawing discrimination in housing and mortgage approvals is not enough, even when the law is fully enforced.

The Urban Institute's Ronald Wienk sums it up this way: "Does housing credit discrimination exist? Yes. Is the behavior of prospective buyers affected by discrimination? Yes. What do we know about credit discrimination and its effects? Very little. Why do we not know very much about housing credit discrimination? Perhaps because we have been searching in the wrong possible places."[19]

Wienk believes that far too little is known about "search behavior," or the way prospective home buyers of different races approach the search for a home and a mortgage. He argues that much more can and should be learned about how lenders treat prospective borrowers when they inquire about financing. The Federal Reserve Bank of Cleveland analyzed the effects of discrimination in four crucial steps in the home-buying process—the initial contact with a real estate agent, the initial contact with a lender, the interaction with the secondary market, and the appraisal of a home's value. The study found that "lenders may discourage potential mortgage customers in a variety of ways, without understanding the potential result"[20] for themselves, in terms of lost business opportunities as well as for customers who are denied a loan. Mortgage officers may discriminate subconsciously—for example, by asking some customers to wait longer than others, talking in industry jargon that the customer doesn't understand, making premature assumptions about minority applicants and thus guiding them to the wrong mortgage product, not reviewing a customer's credit history, collecting inappropriate fees, or offering more options to some applicants than to others.

The appraisal process is another potential vehicle for discrimination. A seller will have difficulty selling a home for more than its appraised value, and a potential buyer won't get financing for a home if the agreed-upon price exceeds the appraised value plus the down payment.

The appraisal process often presents the biggest barrier in central-city neighborhoods that have experienced some decline or deterioration. Low appraisals *can* be the result of neighborhood problems, but even more often they are a contributing factor. Federal Reserve Board governor Lawrence Lindsay, who leads that body's antidiscrimination efforts, observed that "property values in distressed areas seem to be systematically undervalued. The result is to sharply depress the collateral value of inner city properties, thereby cutting them off from lendable funds."[21] When a home is sold at a depressed price because of a low appraisal, the transaction has a ripple effect on the values of other homes. Potential sellers can't get their price; potential buyers can't get their loans; and home owners who want to stay can't get financing for home improvements. The downward spiral accelerates.

The Federal Reserve Bank of Cleveland found that the appraisal process in neighborhoods experiencing complex social and economic changes is inconsistent and highly subjective. Four lenders were asked for appraisals on the same property—a single-family, urban home that was well kept and had undergone significant renovation. The appraisals ranged from $36,000 to $83,500. The appraisal process has to be reformed to eliminate such wide variations. We can no longer afford the disastrous consequences for communities, home owners, and potential buyers of faulty appraisals.

The Boston Federal Reserve study showed that some lenders applied the flexibility in Fannie Mae's underwriting guidelines to white mortgage applicants more often than to minority applicants.[22] Despite the fact that "the provisions of the secondary market guidelines . . . provide various alternative and flexible means by which applicants may demonstrate their ability and willingness to repay their loans,"[23] that flexibility is too seldom applied to minority applicants.

A national strategy for increased home ownership must deal with all sources of discrimination. We have to do more than merely enforce the law, as basic as that is. We have to develop new, effective, positive ways to secure equal access to mortgage credit. We can't just be punitive or reactive.

- The mortgage finance industry must become more diverse, recruiting and training more minorities.

- Lenders, underwriters, appraisers, and real estate agents should be trained to recognize and avoid the subtle and unconscious ways in which they might discriminate against certain customers.

- The federal government, the private sector, and institutions of higher education should develop a cooperative and comprehensive research program on the causes and consequences of racial discrimination in lending.

- The federal government, the private sector, and local antidiscrimination groups should work together to educate consumers about fair housing laws.

- We should prohibit real estate listings that restrict potential buyers' financing options to conventional loans that are not targeted to or appropriate for first-time buyers or low- and moderate-income families.

- We should strengthen minority lenders already in the mortgage finance business by helping them establish the relationships and financial conduits needed to resell their loans in the secondary market.

- We should provide seed capital for expansion to community development lending institutions that operate in minority areas.

- We should reform property appraisal methodologies to more accurately reflect market conditions in urban neighborhoods. Alternatively, we could eliminate the appraisal requirement altogether for properties in distressed central cities.

- The secondary market should conduct a continuing dialogue with lenders to identify underwriting procedures that are confusing or can be misapplied to foster

discrimination, whether intentionally or unintention-
ally. Fannie Mae has already initiated this feedback
process, including providing on-line access to all
underwriting guidelines, regional hotlines which
lenders can call for instant guidance on underwriting,
and an internal loan review board to review applications initially rejected by our underwriters.

One final caution: whatever else we do, whatever new initiatives
we launch, federal law enforcement must play a continuing, fundamental role in the fight against discrimination. The Fair Housing
Act of 1968 plus amendments passed since then constitute a powerful tool for HUD and for the Justice Department. The legal tools
have to be kept in place and in working order. For example, the
Home Mortgage Disclosure Act, by forcing mortgage lenders to disclose their practices and results, has become the basis for objecting
to bank acquisitions where there is evidence of poor community
reinvestment or faulty disclosure practices. Community activist
groups have used the act to delay or stop banks from acquiring new
branches or other banking institutions. It is only because of the federal government that this mortgage data exists at all. To end or limit
such public disclosure would subvert or destroy major private sector attempts to wipe out discrimination.

The Community Reinvestment Act (CRA) has to be kept in
place as well, and it should be improved by new regulations that
streamline its requirements. The CRA requires banks to make loans
in the inner city and to individuals within their service area who
are demonstrably not receiving the credit they need and for which
they qualify. Repealing it now would remove the pressure to make
mortgages available to minorities—and there's no reason to think
that we can afford to dispense with that pressure, that banks would
voluntarily make all the loans they should.

The proper role of Fannie Mae in fighting discrimination is not
in law enforcement but in providing economic incentives. Every

actor in the mortgage finance system, from real estate agents to banks to mortgage bankers, wants to do more business. All of them are anxious to originate a loan if Fannie Mae will agree to buy it. We have made it clear that we accord a high priority to providing more service to African Americans and Hispanics. In 1994 and 1995, Fannie Mae provided $47 billion to finance homes for more than 450,000 minority families.

In the last two years, Fannie Mae has conducted a nationwide search to locate minority-owned mortgage lenders and make each of them a Fannie Mae seller-servicer, which means they can sell loans to Fannie Mae and will be authorized to service those loans. We have almost doubled the number of minority-owned seller-servicers. We are now talking or working with every minority-owned lender in the United States to help them reach the point where they can become an approved seller-servicer.

We also are focusing on the issue of recruitment and training. Fannie Mae is developing a mortgage finance curriculum for community colleges and other institutions to attract minority students and increase the staffing levels of qualified minorities within the home loan industry. We are creating innovative new products with lower down payments and instituting more flexible appraisals of credit histories.

3. Do More to Serve New Immigrants

The millions of new immigrants who will come to the United States in the 1990s and beyond represent more than a growth in population; they are a major new element in the labor market and a key component of the potential home-buying market. Immigration has a particularly strong impact on the first-time-buyer market, because new immigrants tend to be young, with their household-building and child-raising years ahead of them. According to the Census Bureau, 55 percent of recent immigrants are between fifteen and thirty-four years of age, and they typically have more children than their native-born counterparts.[24]

Hispanics constitute a large proportion of new immigrants to the United States, and young renter families account for a disproportionate segment of the nation's Hispanic community. Hispanics tend to live in large households and to be concentrated in metropolitan areas. They are drawn to living in single-family homes. Half of all Hispanic households—and an overwhelming 86 percent of all Hispanic home owners—live in single-family dwellings.[25] They value home ownership and they are ready to make substantial sacrifices to achieve it.

Ana and Alejandro Mendes, the parents of four children, are typical. They immigrated from Mexico and are anxious to obtain U.S. citizenship. Alejandro works as a boat builder and Ana as a homemaker. They owned a home in their native Mexico, and now they yearn to put down roots and become a part of a community of home owners in this country. Ana and Alejandro are working hard to save enough money for a down payment; to economize, they are sharing a rented house with another family.[26]

While immigrants' incomes may be low when they first come to the United States, by the time they have been here for fifteen years, their earnings are on average equal to the average income of native-born Americans.[27] The home ownership rate for foreign-born individuals who have lived in the United States for ten to twenty years approaches—and among some groups surpasses—the rate for the nation as a whole.[28]

For most immigrants who arrived in the 1980s or later, however, the road to home ownership will be a longer one. Immigrants' earning power is growing at a slower pace than in the past. In part this reflects the fact that the newer immigrants tend to have less formal education than immigrants in earlier decades. They aren't prepared for anything other than low-skill jobs, which is much more of a handicap in today's high-tech economy than it was for earlier immigrants. On average, a new immigrant earned 32 percent less than a native-born American in 1990; in 1970 the figure was only 17 percent. By 1990 the incomes of immigrants who arrived in the late 1970s were still 16 percent lower than those of nonimmigrants. In contrast, many immigrants who came to the United States in the early 1960s have caught up and subsequently surpassed their native-born counterparts.[29]

Aggressive outreach to new immigrants is vital to any strategy to increase home ownership.

- Those in the process of becoming citizens should be automatically exposed to the process of becoming home owners. The Immigration and Naturalization Service (INS) and the housing finance industry should establish linkages to ensure that new immigrants studying to become citizens receive consumer information to help them understand the home-buying process and find opportunities for home ownership.

- We must provide this information in immigrants' native languages. According to the 1990 Census, almost thirty-two million people living in the United States speak a language other than English at home; in almost three million households, no one speaks English. The housing finance industry and real estate agents should advertise in languages other than English and conduct housing fairs and other outreach activities in multiple languages.

- We should train lenders and real estate professionals to help them understand cultural differences that affect the home-buying process. For example, some Asian home buyers choose homes based on the principles of *feng shui*, which governs the shape and orientation of rooms and teaches them to avoid homes on busy streets or at intersections. Some Latinos, on the other hand, prefer brick homes on major streets; they like access to public transportation, and they tend to regard wooden homes as insubstantial. We must also take cultural differences into account in loan underwriting.

> While most lenders are familiar with the practice of
> using a gift from parents to help with a down payment,
> in many immigrant cultures, the extended family—
> cousins, aunts, uncles, in-laws—will pool their
> resources to help a family member buy a home.
> Verification of the source of such funds is almost
> impossible, but it is as valid as the traditional gift
> from parents.

Citizenship and home ownership are a potent combination right now because of the high number of immigrants who are eligible to become citizens as a result of the immigration reform legislation of 1986. That law granted amnesty to all those who had been residing in the United States illegally since January 1, 1982. As a result, about 3.1 million people became permanent residents of the United States.[30] All of them, along with 2.4 million immigrants who achieved permanent residency status through the regular process, will be eligible for citizenship by 1996.

We need these 5.5 million potential citizens. They can be a powerful source of vitality and stability in our distressed inner cities. Mayors across the country have told me time and time again how immigrants are bringing decaying neighborhoods back to life through their energy, their entrepreneurship, and their commitment to family and faith.

In Boston, immigration is the only source of population growth; despite a drop in the white population of 11 percent in the 1980s, the overall population of the city increased. In 1900, as the century began, Boston's Dorchester neighborhood was home to two hundred thousand people—70 percent of them foreign-born immigrants from Ireland, the Balkans, and Southern Europe. Today, as the century nears its end, Dorchester is still an immigrant community, the home to Vietnamese immigrants, Haitians, Cambodians, Dominicans, Cape Verdeans, Thais, and new Irish immigrants, for whom Boston is still a magnet.

The great journalist Theodore White once observed that the waves of immigration coming to Boston were an "ethnic ballet, slow yet certain."[31] As if to confirm that analysis, Jose Vincenty, a Puerto Rican lawyer and community activist, told the *Boston Globe* in 1993 that the city's Latino community "[has much] in common with the old Irish and Italian immigrants, because of the issue of family values. They want to work hard and make it in the new country. The issue of church and parental involvement in the child's life is very important."[32]

The *Globe* reported that newcomers to Boston are being welcomed by longtime residents, who "nod approvingly" as the immigrants "purchase their own home, open their own businesses, and even send their children to parochial school." Businesses are booming in Dorchester, and a local social service agency, the Federated Dorchester Neighborhood Houses, found that 80 percent of the new businesses—and 100 percent of the new Vietnamese-owned businesses—were started with the owner's personal savings or the savings of a family member. One leading worker predicted that "our new wave of immigrants are the Massachusetts miracle of the year 2010. They are our economic base."[33]

In Oakland, California, which suffered a devastating earthquake in 1989 and then a deep recession, immigrants are the leading edge of an economic comeback. Since the 1980s, a declining Chinatown has become a thriving "Asiatown" with the "energetic infusion of entrepreneurial Southeast Asian refugees," including Filipinos, Koreans, Laotians, Chinese, and Vietnamese.[34] New York City, long the heartland of immigration, is more diverse than ever, and the city is reaping the benefits in neighborhood revitalization, higher consumer spending, new job creation, and increased tax receipts. "Immigrants contribute to the general well-being here," notes the director of New York's Office of Immigrant Affairs. "Immigration keeps our [population] numbers up, keeps businesses going, helps revitalize neighborhoods. . . . [Immigrants] may work long hours under difficult conditions, but they *are* working."[35]

The central cities aren't the only places where immigrants go in search of the American dream. More than three hundred thousand people now reside in the shanties they have built for themselves in the *colonias*, the rural unincorporated communities on the Texas side of the U.S.-Mexican border. These communities lack basic services like sewer, water, and electricity; here, home ownership seems a distant dream. But through the work of the immigrants themselves, along with local governments and nonprofit institutions (including the Fannie Mae Foundation), primitive conditions are being succeeded by new opportunities for decent housing and home ownership.

This nation of home owners is also, in President Kennedy's words, "a nation of immigrants." Our national character has been shaped by the courage, talent, ideals, and capacity for hard work that our forebears brought with them from their native lands. Now immigrants from Latin America, Asia, Africa, and the Caribbean are coming to America with the same ambition as the Europeans who came before—to make a better life for themselves and their children. The newcomers bring with them a fierce determination to earn and save, to educate the next generation, and to practice their faith with freedom and respect. In the borough of Queens, New York, Hindu and Buddhist temples have sprung up beside Roman Catholic churches and Jewish synagogues. Roger Rosenblatt examined the settlement of new immigrants in Brooklyn's Sunset Park neighborhood for *The New Republic:* "Like their predecessors, the new immigrants came to Sunset Park and to America to find work, though there was much less available; to establish and rear families, and in some cases, to escape political oppression. . . . Most, too, are strong advocates of family cohesion, though some have seen their own families disintegrate in America, and realize that they have entered a civilization where families have been coming apart for decades. Most have retained formal religion. Most are dismayed at the quality of the schools; and most have no use for bilingual education."[36]

Rosenblatt found that the immigrants had improved the area's intellectual life, opening bookstores and paying close attention to local schools: "neighborhood educators believe the schools will only get better if more immigrants enroll." Immigrants are also improving Sunset Park's economy with new shops and row upon row of rehabbed houses. Rosenblatt wrote that immigrant attitudes toward work "border on the zealous. . . . Asians in the neighborhood sound no different discussing their work than any middle Europeans of the 1920s—the same mixture of purposefulness and humorless ambition."[37]

Despite (and perhaps because of) such success, we have recently seen the rise of a new nativism. It feeds on an almost pathological fear of newcomers, turning them into scapegoats for social ills and demanding that we slam the door on future immigration. The reaction hit first in California, a state that attracts more immigrants than any other. In 1994, voters overwhelmingly approved Proposition 187, a measure designed to deny education, social services, and health care to those who cannot prove their legal right to be in the United States. The measure has not yet taken effect because of a restraining order issued by the U.S. District Court. If it were to be implemented, children would be denied the chance to go to school or to see a doctor when they're sick. The reaction has already spread to legal immigrants, with new calls in Congress to cut off all immigration and to institute new policies that would withhold federal benefits even from legal immigrants who are not yet citizens.

The reaction is not only an ugly one, it is contrary to our national character and history. And it is wrong not only morally but also economically. Michael Fix and Jeffrey Passel of the Urban Institute have found that far from being a drain on taxpayers, working-class immigrants make a positive contribution to the Treasury, paying much more in federal taxes than they receive in federal benefits.[38] And the contributions become greater as immigrants become citizens. Naturalized citizens are more likely than Americans in general to generate economic growth, expand the tax base, join in community development efforts, and be active in public affairs. Over

90 percent of naturalized citizens register to vote, far above the rate of native-born Americans.[39]

Unfortunately, the naturalization process suffers from some of the same weaknesses as the home-buying process. Danny Solis, of the United Neighborhood Organization of Chicago (UNO), argues that it's harder than it's supposed to be to become a citizen: "People are not invited into the process nor is the process inviting." Potential applicants for citizenship face administrative delays and often feel a sense of intimidation. During previous waves of immigration to the United States, Solis observes that "a greater collaborative effort existed between the Immigration and Naturalization Service and the institutions [such as civic groups, unions, and churches]. . . . Potential citizens were wooed into the 'Americanization' process."[40]

As a nation, we have to return to the days of "wooing" immigrants, inviting them to become citizens—and while we're at it, we should "woo" them into buying homes as well. UNO has worked with the INS in Chicago to pioneer a community partnership dedicated to telling potential citizens in their native language how to become citizens. Churches have played an important role in this partnership, and Fannie Mae has been involved from the start.

Fannie Mae has cosponsored home ownership and citizenship fairs with UNO; these programs have been a model for our outreach efforts around the nation. At the fairs, newly naturalized citizens, potential citizens, and potential home owners asked questions and collected material from the INS, the Social Security Administration, and the local voter-registration board. Fannie Mae offered information in seven languages about how to buy a home, along with a list of local lenders committed to working with immigrant home buyers.

Fluvia and Sergio Ramos attended one such fair. Fluvia, a telephone customer service administrator, was born in Chicago. But her husband, Sergio, a native of Guatemala, had only been in the United States for seven years. Sergio was a new citizen. After living in rental housing for many years, they wanted to buy a home. Although both Ramoses speak English, Sergio felt more confident in his native Spanish, especially when dealing with complicated financial matters. They attended a bilingual housing fair sponsored by Fannie Mae. With the material they found at the fair and a new-found sense of confidence about the subtleties of the mortgage process, the couple approached a lender to ask about buying a three-bedroom brick bungalow. "The loan process was just what we expected," Mrs. Ramos said. "The brochures told us what kind of loans were available and helped us to understand the market."[41]

The reasons to focus on new immigrants are obvious: they're motivated, and they have a higher savings rate. When you compare the savings rate among immigrants and nonimmigrants, you can see where the immigrants get the down payment for housing. They mostly get it the old-fashioned way: they and their extended families save for it. In the 1980s and 1990s, there will be a total of sixteen million new legal immigrants to the United States. They will become the biggest single element affecting the overall middle-class housing demand.

4. Help Those Who Don't Initially Qualify

It's profoundly discouraging for a family to go through the arduous process of applying for a mortgage, to feel the hope and excitement of buying a new home, and then be turned down. They may give up without ever knowing that a decision by one lender to deny them a mortgage is neither permanent nor irreversible.

Alina Parapar is someone who didn't give up. A mother of five—two daughters and three stepsons—Parapar was fiercely determined to own a home. When she found the house of her dreams in Miami's West Kendall neighborhood, she simply wasn't going to take no for an answer. The property, a single-family home with three bedrooms in a quiet neighborhood with good schools, was for sale as the result of a foreclosure—and that made the price affordable. But Parapar faced an obstacle—a damaged credit history because of her first husband's unpaid debts. Her loan application was denied by the institution that held the foreclosed property.

Too many prospective home owners would stop right there— disappointed and frustrated, thinking there was nowhere to turn. But Parapar worked at one of Miami's largest hotels, which just happened to be the site of a major home buyer fair sponsored by Fannie Mae. She picked up a copy of our step-by-step guide to home buying. She spoke to a Fannie Mae staff member about her situation and was told how to try again. She went back to the lender and showed that she had built a responsible credit record of her own, even voluntarily assuming payments on some of her former husband's debts. This time she won a conventional mortgage on her West Miami dream home.

"I honestly couldn't have done it without the information I got from Fannie Mae," Ms. Parapar said later. "I was totally unaware that I could turn things around. I suggested to the lender some of the things I saw in the [Fannie Mae] pamphlet—the fact that I was buying on my own; I was a female with kids; a working mother."[42]

Counseling agencies offer an array of services that provide information and advice similar to what Alina Parapar received at the Fannie Mae housing fair. The agencies tell people the maximum mortgage for which they can qualify, what they need for a down payment, and how much closing costs are likely to run. The agencies identify the low down payment options offered by local lenders, who like to do business with the graduates of home buyer counseling programs. The programs are a reliable link between a potential buyer and institutions that provide funds to finance home purchases. For families not quite ready to buy, counseling agencies offer classes on credit and budgeting and work one-on-one with each family to develop a plan to correct past credit problems and solve other difficulties that may lead a lender to turn down a loan.

At Fannie Mae, we believe that home ownership counseling also makes it less likely that a borrower will fall into delinquency or default on a mortgage obligation. The statistical evidence is inconclusive, but it points in that direction. So Fannie Mae requires counseling as a precondition for some of the low down payment loans we finance for low- and moderate-income families. Such loans perform better than loans to similarly situated buyers who haven't received counseling.

National and local grassroots organizations have been running successful home ownership programs for many years. These programs target low- and moderate-income families for counseling, usually first-time buyers and people who have had credit problems in the past (or no credit at all). The Organization for a New Equality has made home ownership counseling part of its Campaign for Economic Literacy in Boston; as a result, hundreds of families have taken steps to improve their credit rating. Catholic Charities USA and the Neighborhood Reinvestment Corporation also operate consumer education and home buyer counseling in major metropolitan areas. The Fannie Mae Foundation has a major commitment to support these efforts.

Home buyer education today is decentralized, fragmented, and uncoordinated. As the demand for counseling increases and its success becomes more evident, a national home ownership strategy must make home buyer education available to all potential buyers, no matter where they live. This will require financial support from both the federal government and the housing finance industry.

- Every home-buying counseling agency needs new technologies to improve services and increase the number of consumers served. Fannie Mae has developed a software program—Desktop Home Counselor—that helps agencies and prospective home owners quickly determine their eligibility for a spectrum of mortgage products. In 1994 we piloted Desktop Home Counselor with forty nonprofits and ten private sector lenders, and in 1995 we distributed an enhanced version to a network of 175 counselors and lenders. By 1997 we will have made Desktop Home Counselor universally available to lenders and nonprofit counseling agencies.

- A new National Center for Home Buyer Education, modeled on the National Center for Lead Safe Housing (established by Fannie Mae in 1992), should develop and distribute model curricula, training programs, and educational materials to the counseling agencies. The center should set performance standards for the industry and implement certification standards for counselors.

- Because most home buyer education agencies are located in metropolitan areas, a national toll-free phone number should be available to callers from rural areas who want to know where to turn. We should direct special efforts toward minority communities that have lacked such counseling in the past, and toward people for whom English is not their first language. All lenders should agree to take a "second look" at mortgage applications they have denied to see if there are innovative ways to qualify marginal applicants, and they should agree to advise clients on what they need to do to change "no" to "yes." The vast majority of lenders—88 percent—already have some type of "second review" program in place that automatically double-checks rejected applications. Federal regulators also suggest that banks implement internal "second look" programs to promote compliance with fair lending laws. The suggestion should become a requirement.

- Third-party reviews should become an integral part of the mortgage application process. A group composed of both outside experts and professionals from within the lending institution should reexamine rejected mortgage applications. A "fresh set of eyes" can often make an approval feasible.

The most important single determinant of the viability of a mortgage for borderline applicants is not their capacity to pay, although that is properly and inevitably part of the equation. The single most important factor is their commitment to pay. That commitment can be hard to prove, and its intensity can be even harder to measure. Angelo Mozilo, the CEO of Countrywide Home Loans and one of the mortgage industry's most farsighted leaders, has urged mortgage institutions to welcome and prize home buyers who say (and mean it), "We are so thrilled to own our own home that we are horrified by the notion that we could lose it. We will make enormous sacrifices—take additional jobs, ask members of our family to contribute to the mortgage, sacrifice in other areas, cut back our consumption and expenditures. But we will not fail." That, in the end, is the real definition of a good risk. But if an applicant's financial situation is borderline, if the future market value of the house the applicant wants to buy is threatened because it is in a troubled neighborhood or a declining market, if there is uncertainty about the applicant's commitment to pay, then there is also a great risk of failure.

At Fannie Mae, we are consciously using our enormous capacity and influence in the home mortgage system to help lenders hone their ability to calculate the likelihood of making a successful loan to those who have been or might be denied. We are seeking, in concert with lenders and other institutions, to open a dialogue with every potential home buyer who has some real likelihood of success in paying off a mortgage.

As we've noted before, there are millions of people today who are economically qualified to own a home but don't. There are millions of people who are mortgage-eligible but don't know it. There is a daunting information barrier and an endemic discrimination barrier. In the end, if we can refine the dialogue we have with such families, we can assist them in achieving home ownership in a way that will benefit communities, benefit American society, and create new equity in new homes. These mortgages will be overwhelmingly successful; they will perform.

All this points toward mining a vein of commitment that seems to be extraordinarily deep and strong in this nation—the notion of owning a home, the idea that your family can build a financial asset of remarkable quality. Virtually no other type of credit performs as well as a home mortgage; corporate lines of credit, small business loans, credit cards—all these other credit mechanisms pale in comparison to the credit performance of mortgages. This, in my view, reflects the greatest value of owning a home, the value that goes deeper than dollars—providing a safe and secure environment for a family, a place of their own. One of our priorities as a society, one of the imperatives of our political leadership, must be to advance this value and deliver the kind of commitment that can make it real. This is vital, not just to expand home ownership but to restore the well-being of the country.

5. Create More Incentives to Save

All the studies—including Fannie Mae's *National Housing Survey* and a survey of members of the Mortgage Bankers Association of America released in March 1994—show that the single biggest barrier to home ownership for first-time buyers who are otherwise economically qualified is lack of savings for a down payment.[43] According to the Joint Center for Housing Studies, fewer than one-third of young renter households have enough cash to cover both a 10 percent down payment and the closing cost for a typical starter home. In fact, the net wealth of a typical renter household in 1993 was equal to just one-third of the cost of a 10 percent down payment and closing costs.[44]

More specifically, home ownership rates among young married couples have been declining for more than ten years. This is particularly troubling, since marriage itself has usually facilitated purchasing a home. Most families who manage to become home owners accumulate the funds for the down payment during the two years prior to purchase. The rapid accumulation of wealth is often made possible by marriage, which in effect doubles the wealth of the household. Many married women also go to work just before they and their husbands decide to buy, and they remain in the work force long afterward.[45]

Another important source of funds for a down payment is gifts and inheritances, which average 15 percent of the value of houses purchased by young households.[46] One analysis of survey data on home buying compiled by the Chicago Title and Trust Company found that 22 percent of all first-time home buyers receive a gift to help with the down payment that averages more than half of what is required. Those who rely on gifts have lower incomes and higher expenses; both spouses are more likely to work outside the home. Gifts allow them to buy earlier than they could on their own and to buy a more expensive home.[47]

How closely do home and marriage go together? Only about 40 percent of female-headed households own homes, while the rate for married couples reaches into the upper 70 percent range. In fact, nearly half of female-headed households report having no savings at all, compared to one-third of male-headed households and one-quarter of married couples. Furthermore, nine out of ten women in this situation report that the lack of cash for a down payment—even a "low" 3 or 5 percent down payment—is the principal reason why they can't buy a home.[48]

Any effective strategy to increase home ownership must include incentives for young families to save for the express purpose of buying their first house.

- Tax laws should permit first-time home buyers to withdraw funds from tax-deferred Individual Retirement Accounts and other retirement savings plans to invest in a down payment.

- Financial institutions should offer contract savings for housing (CSH) programs, through which low- and moderate-income families deposit savings in a home ownership account in exchange for a commitment from a financial institution to provide a mortgage, on prearranged terms, for a home purchase for which they otherwise qualify.

There are a number of ways such programs could be structured. The interest earned on the savings could be made tax free. Interest rate subsidies could assure mortgage loans that are affordable. In Great Britain, potential home buyers contract with "building associations"—similar to our S&Ls—to save a specified amount each month for five years. At the end of five years, the government adds a bonus equal to fourteen months' worth of savings; if the family continues to save for another two years, the government doubles the bonus. All the interest earned on the savings is tax-free. Germany and France also have extensive experience with CSH programs, which have brought an increase in both the savings and home ownership rates of their low-income families.[49] Some lenders in the United States have experimented with contract savings plans as well; the greatest limit on them is the lack of any public subsidies for tax exemptions.

CSH programs provide a powerful inducement for saving: those who save as promised are guaranteed a mortgage. CSH programs also help lending institutions locate good credit risks among households that might lack traditional qualifications for a conventional loan. By linking low-income families with financial institutions, the programs generate both new business for banks and more access to financial services for consumers of modest means. At the same time, lenders learn to be responsive to the needs of a whole new group of customers. Encouraging more savings is one answer for those who lack the savings for a down payment and closing costs but otherwise might qualify for a loan. Still, this is only half a solution.

6. Make Low Down Payment Mortgages Broadly Available to First-Time Buyers

A comprehensive study of housing affordability between 1960 and 1989 found that the "inherent wealth constraints embedded in the down payment requirements" deny home ownership to many families who could readily afford the monthly payment.[50]

Brian Cowan and his wife, Lynne Jerome, lived in a high-cost market in California, with home prices far above the national average. They thought they would have to be "close to retirement" before they were able to save enough for a down payment. Brian, a waiter, and Lynne, an office manager and student, couldn't accumulate enough savings on their combined income of about $33,000 to bring home ownership within their reach: "We always paid a lot of money per month in rent—probably comparable to a mortgage payment, but instead of a mortgage, we took out student loans to cover school expenses," Lynne said. "We hated throwing money down the drain in rent, and couldn't see the benefits of paying rent in the long term. We always took as much care of the property we rented as we would our own home. Every time we would go outside and work in the yard, or paint a room, it made us cringe because we could have been doing it for our own place."[51]

Brian and Lynne are typical of many young families who want to buy their first home. Their story has a happy ending, because they were able to qualify for a low down payment mortgage under the Fannie Mae Community Home Buyer's Program, which offers the "3/2 option." They put a 3 percent down payment on a $163,500 home in Oakland's Maxwell Park neighborhood. The city of Oakland contributed the remaining 2 percent, along with a mortgage assistance grant of $35,000, which allowed the couple to qualify for the home they wanted. In exchange for the financial assistance, Brian and Lynne completed home ownership counseling, which helps first-time buyers understand and plan for the responsibility of owning a home.

ACORN and Fannie Mae have launched a pilot program in sixteen cities, through which potential home buyers who go through ACORN's counseling program can qualify for mortgages with a down payment of $1,000 or 3 percent of the purchase price, whichever is less. Other nonprofit organizations, as well as a number of local governments, are providing grants to low- and moderate-income home buyers to add to their own savings so they can afford a down payment.

First-time home buyers short of savings are also turning to the Federal Housing Administration (FHA), the most important source of low down payment loans. Borrowers who get FHA-insured loans can put down 5 percent or less of the purchase price of a modest home; the limit is a home valued at $152,362. FHA loans have another big benefit—the borrower can finance the closing costs as well as the purchase price. This represents a major reduction in the cash required to complete the transaction.

Some lenders have experimented with zero down payment loans that carry no government guarantee. A no down payment loan is riskier for both the borrower and the lender. Because of the way mortgages are amortized, a borrower with a zero down payment mortgage will have very little equity in the home for years to come. If the home owner experiences a period of financial distress, there's minimal incentive against defaulting on the mortgage. The lender could be left with the property, and the borrower could find it almost impossible to buy another home in the future.

There are other very low down payment options. Under a lease purchase plan, a prospective home owner contracts with a seller to rent a house for a specified period of time; they agree that part of the rent will be set aside as a down payment. At the end of the lease, the renter can qualify for a mortgage loan with all or most of his down payment already made. Some lenders have offered innovative lease-purchase programs on properties obtained as a result of foreclosure. In Aberdeen, Washington, Anchor Mutual Savings Bank designed just such a program to market more than one hundred single-family homes it owned. The bank would negotiate a sales price for a property with a qualified low- or moderate-income family and then set a lease rate at an amount equal to a mortgage payment for that price. The family leasing the property could then accumulate a 10 percent down payment through sweat equity, home improvements, or savings. Once the family had the down payment, the bank approved the mortgage and the transition from renting to owning.[52]

"Sweat equity" is an important path to home ownership. A home buyer who agrees to rehabilitate a dilapidated property can offer hard work instead of cash for a down payment. Homestead programs that rely on sweat equity have proved successful in depressed urban neighborhoods where abandoned properties are owned by lending institutions, the city, or the federal government.

Tax-exempt mortgage revenue bonds (MRBs) also open the door to home ownership. The bonds carry below-market interest rates: local and state housing finance agencies issue them to provide mortgage assistance to low- and moderate-income first-time home buyers with incomes no more than 115 percent of the median income for the area. The National Association of Home Builders estimates that MRBs make possible 130,000 first-time home purchases a year.[53]

A low down payment loan isn't always the best option. Establishing equity right from the start, so the buyer has a stake in the house from the first day, is one important way to reduce the lender's risk. Default is expensive for everyone—lenders, insurers, investors, communities, and taxpayers. It is most expensive, and tragic, for the family that loses their home. We aren't doing anyone a favor when we give people mortgages they can't afford. But most low down payment loans don't default.

Mortgages originated in 1982, during a deep recession, have the worst performance record to date. But even for these mortgages, for every borrower with a loan-to-value ratio of 90 percent who lost his home, there were nine borrowers with similar mortgage terms who did not.[54] The cost to the nation and to the economy of not making these loans would be dramatic, producing a major downturn in the housing sector. In the 1980s, over four million families financed their homes with down payments of 10 percent or less; over ten million made down payments of less than 20 percent.[55]

A strategy for increased home ownership must include ways of expanding low down payment options.

- We must expand risk sharing among financially capable partners. For more than thirty years, lenders and private mortgage insurance companies have worked together to manage the risks of low down payment lending. The industry should now focus on risk sharing within a wider universe, through innovative mortgage financing that combines the resources of the federal government, the FHA, nonprofit institutions, state agencies, mortgage lenders, a borrower's family, and local government. The partnership between Fannie Mae and the city of Oakland that resulted in a home for Brian Cowan and Lynne Jerome is a good example of risk sharing. Low down payment programs should specifically target families who otherwise couldn't buy a home, not those who have sufficient savings and income but simply prefer a low down payment mortgage.

- We must continually revise and update underwriting standards to recognize the higher risks as well as the unique circumstances of low down payment loans. For example, first-time buyers rarely have well-established credit histories, but they can be permitted to demonstrate creditworthiness with a consistently timely payment of rent and utilities.

- Geographic diversification, provided by the secondary market, is essential. We have to insulate the housing finance system as much as possible from the effects of regional economic distress. For example, although regional recessions have caused higher delinquencies and foreclosures in the Northeast and the West in the past few years, during the same period, Fannie Mae's loan performance in other parts of the country has been good. Only because we operate in a national market can we weather periodic regional downturns.

- The housing finance industry must invest in research, development, and experimentation. Underwriting standards should be continually revalidated and changed to ensure that creditworthy applicants aren't being turned away. Credit history, down payment amounts and sources, debt-to-income ratios, borrower income, and the appraisal process are all factors to be tested as part of our effort to design innovative products to expand home ownership.

- Early intervention in delinquencies can mitigate losses. Delinquency prevention and foreclosure avoidance strategies can help keep borrowers who are in financial trouble in their own homes by modifying loan terms— for example, by refinancing the loan from an above-market rate to a market rate.

- Prepurchase counseling can help potential home buyers assess their credit, repair it where necessary, and learn to manage money effectively to prevent delinquency and default. Postpurchase counseling can provide an early warning system for discovering potential delinquencies.

7. Invest in New Technology to Shorten the Application Process and Make Origination Less Expensive

The housing finance industry is in the first stages of a technological revolution. While other industries were computerizing, mortgage lenders largely refused to leave the dark ages. This has only just begun to change. In the securities industry, millions of dollars can be moved with the touch of a button. In the mortgage industry, money, data, and paper—reams and reams of paper—are moved manually through an origination process that can take months to complete.

This inefficiency is, of course, expensive. It costs a lender about $2,500 to originate a mortgage loan. For a conventional thirty-year mortgage for $100,000, a borrower's closing costs can amount to more than 6.5 percent of the loan amount. These costs are a real barrier to home ownership for millions of Americans.

A national home ownership strategy must include bringing the housing finance industry fully into the computer age. We need to apply new technologies to the most complex phases in the creation of the mortgage asset—origination, underwriting, and secondary marketing.

Our goal at Fannie Mae is to cut at least $1,000 from the cost of making a mortgage and to reduce origination time from eight weeks, or longer, to five days. We hear a lot about the promise of the "information superhighway"; at Fannie Mae, we are building such a highway to link the various components of the mortgage finance industry. We are doing it in partnership with lenders. We surveyed them to find out what they need to improve their services and to reach more potential home buyers. They wanted open systems that would simplify their work, systems flexible enough to be navigated with existing software. Then we examined the entire loan life cycle, from the time the borrower thinks about getting a loan until it gets sold to a Wall Street investor.

With all this as a foundation, we are leveraging our technology investments to reengineer the way the housing finance industry does business. We have introduced new software systems and an on-line financial services network. We have completely automated the origination and underwriting process. Our mortgage origination process, once choked by volumes of paper containing information that had to be entered and reentered into the system many times (with many opportunities for errors), is now paperless. Our new technologies are compatible with the computer systems that lenders already have in their offices; they will work for all mortgages and are available to everyone in the industry. They will work on any personal computer; they are so comprehensible that even a first-time user can be prompted through the system and operate it effectively.

For example, I referred to our Desktop Home Counselor earlier in this chapter; it's a software tool that helps housing counselors and prospective home buyers evaluate their credit and determine how much they can afford to spend on a home. It accesses credit bureau information instantly to give borrowers accurate information about where they stand and what they need to do to qualify for a loan. By helping prepare home buyers for the mortgage application process before they apply, Desktop Home Counselor makes it easier, and more profitable, for lenders to serve applicants who don't fit a "cookie-cutter" profile.

Desktop Originator is another innovation that affects the application process. It lets the mortgage originator take applications in a matter of minutes, qualify a borrower for a loan, lock in a mortgage rate, and communicate directly with lenders. The borrower can secure an immediate response.

Desktop Underwriter uses artificial intelligence to evaluate a mortgage loan application. It analyzes an applicant's finances and the characteristics of the property being purchased, relying on Fannie Mae underwriting guidelines to make a decision about whether a loan can be approved. Borrowers will receive clear and consistent information about underwriting decisions. Underwriters will be free to spend more time on difficult cases.

Electronic data interchange (EDI) programs are also automating the mortgage industry by providing an electronic link between lenders and all their business partners—appraisers, mortgage insurers, title companies, hazard insurers, credit agencies, and the secondary market. Fannie Mae's EDI system provides a link to more than 5,400 subscribers, giving them instant access to a wide array of services, reduced costs, and improved opportunities to streamline operations.

Computer technology is now creating an electronic registry of mortgage ownership for the entire industry. Frequently mortgage documents are transferred after closing, as the loans and/or their servicing rights are moved within the industry. By adopting an electronic "whole loan book entry" system, the actual mortgage note can be permanently stored with a custodian. Transfers can then be registered electronically, eliminating the need for all the streams of paper now crisscrossing the system.

As lenders process more applications more quickly and efficiently, the cost of originating a mortgage will drop dramatically. Given the highly competitive nature of the mortgage finance industry, the bulk of the savings will be passed on to borrowers in the form of lower closing costs.

Borrowers will benefit as well from increased speed in evaluating their applications and less uncertainty as interest rates fluctuate. Furthermore, underwriters will be freed from the tedious and time-consuming process of looking at each application from the ground up, giving them more time to work with borrowers who face unusual circumstances or need more help in order to qualify.

Joyce and Amos Edwards needed that kind of extra help, and a lender in their hometown of San Diego spent the time to make their home ownership dream come true. Amos, the owner of a janitorial service, and Joyce, a city parking-enforcement officer, hoped to buy a home in the Spring Valley neighborhood of San Diego, where they were renting an apartment. They qualified for a low down payment mortgage offered by Fannie Mae; the Edwardses provided a 3 percent down payment, and a gift from a relative provided the remaining 2 percent. But they didn't anticipate the obstacles they would face in trying to complete their purchase.

Because Amos Edwards is self-employed, it took time to document his income. An apparent blemish on their credit rating could have stalled the process, but the Edwardses were able to satisfy the questions the underwriters had. Finally, they were turned down by two mortgage insurance companies. But their lender was persistent and identified a company that would insure the property. Eventually the loan closed; the couple's monthly payment of $905 is less than they were paying in rent.

Joyce Edwards's advice for others who run into trouble when they want to buy a house: "Don't give up. Just try, try, try."[56] But the lender has to try as well; the Edwardses' lending institution could have given up on them because their case was harder than usual. New technologies mean more lenders can devote more time and resources to cases like this. Technology can bring home ownership within reach for families who otherwise would be routinely denied mortgage credit, without a second look.

8. Develop New Ways to Finance Home Ownership

In the city of Boston there are many two- and three-family properties. In New York City, co-ops are common. Native Americans living on reservations may own their homes but hold the land they're built on in common. Central-city home buyers may need financing for rehabbing as well as purchase. And in rural areas, a single-family property can be anything from a house on a small lot to a multiacre lot that contains barns and outbuildings in addition to a home.

Like most industries, the housing finance industry has sought to standardize its products to promote efficiency and reduce costs. But a home is as individual as the family who owns it, and financing options have to be customized as well.

Take the case of James and Ruth Waldie. Like many older Americans, they were house rich and cash poor. They thought they would have to sell the Colorado home they had lived in for twenty-seven years to finance the retirement they had worked for during their fifty-year marriage. But the availability of an innovative mortgage product let them have both their retirement and their home. The Waldies obtained a reverse-annuity mortgage, which gives them a monthly payment, based on the $130,000 equity in their home, to supplement the pension that James, age seventy-eight, earned from the Rio Grande Railroad and Ruth, age eighty-two, earned from her years as a schoolteacher. At no time will the Waldies lose their home; it is theirs until they sell it, move away, or die. The reverse-annuity mortgage simply lets them reap the benefit of their investment, while still living in the house they have called home for more than a quarter of a century.[57]

A reverse-annuity mortgage is just one of dozens of customized mortgage products that can help American families attain—and, in the case of people like James and Ruth Waldie, maintain—home ownership. Energy-efficiency mortgages are another example. Every home owner knows that the monthly cost of housing involves more than a mortgage payment. Utilities can represent as much as 20 percent of total housing costs—enough to put home ownership out of reach for many lower-income families. The U.S. Department of Energy estimates that households earning between $20,000 and $35,000 spend twice as high a percentage of their income on utility expenses as households earning $50,000 or more.[58] The Alliance to Save Energy concluded that if the energy costs of a typical house were reduced by 25 percent, an additional two million families would qualify to buy a home.[59] An energy-efficiency mortgage helps borrowers qualify for a mortgage by taking into account the lower energy bills a home owner will have as a result of buying an energy-efficient home. An energy-efficient mortgage can also cover the costs of making home improvements that reduce energy costs.

Our highest priority should be to develop new mortgage products that reach people and communities that have been underserved in the past—including rural areas, Native Americans, and the elderly. We need types of mortgages that encourage home improvements and rehabilitation, energy efficiency, and new construction of affordable housing.

9. Expand Community Partnerships and Leverage the Contributions of Nonprofit Organizations

Norma Holy Bear grew up in a large foster home on the Sioux Indian reservation in Eagle Butte, South Dakota. Now 29, Holy Bear, a commercial cook, is the mother of two small children. Until recently the family lived with a friend in an efficiency apartment in the Sioux homeland. A community partnership between the Fannie Mae Foundation, the Sioux reservation, and the nonprofit foundation Habitat for Humanity changed all that. Norma Holy Bear and her daughters now live in a three-bedroom home on the reservation, built as part of an effort to bring home ownership to thirty Native American families in Eagle Butte.

It won't be easy to achieve this goal. The average income for a family of four in Eagle Butte is $19,000. Holy Bear, who is single, has an annual income of just $13,000. To qualify for her home, she had to make a down payment of $700 and put five hundred hours' worth of "sweat equity" into the houses in the Habitat for Humanity development. In addition, Norma Holy Bear was required to complete home ownership counseling. As a result, she says, "I am being more responsible; trying to manage my bills better, and keeping my home better."[60] Home ownership would be out of reach for people like Norma Holy Bear and her children without such public-private partnerships.

These partnerships are at least as critical in the central cities, where opportunities for home ownership steadily declined between 1960 and 1990. Anthony Downs of the Brookings Institution identifies two types of inner-city neighborhoods:

> Stagnant or declining neighborhoods have stable or falling populations, decreasing local employment, and are mainly black. Because they are gradually emptying out as people who can afford to live elsewhere move away, they often contain abandoned housing and large tracts of vacant cleared land. . . . Dynamic and still-growing neighborhoods have increasing population because of immigration, but stable levels of local employment and mainly Hispanic and Asian residents, though some contain many black residents too. These neighborhoods are usually overcrowded; they contain few vacant housing units, and many units designed for one household are occupied by two or more. Even though people who can afford to live elsewhere often move out, they are immediately replaced by new immigrants.[61]

Downs notes that both types of neighborhoods face social conditions that threaten the "economic prosperity and political viability of American society . . . a lack of civil order, poverty among children, poor public education, and incomplete integration of workers into the economy."[62]

An expansion of home ownership is certainly not a cure-all; the causes of inner-city decline are complex. They are "rooted in certain persistent long-range social trends that many people regard as desirable. These include rising real incomes, greater use of cars and trucks, widespread desire for living in relatively new low-density settlements, economic advantages of homeownership, and strongly entrenched tendencies for people to segregate themselves socio-economically and racially by neighborhood."[63] The expansion of computer technology and electronic communications and the decline of manufacturing jobs contribute to the flight from the inner city as well.

But unless we bring home ownership and its civic benefits back to the central city, we will not only hollow out our great urban centers, we will magnify the crises of crime, discrimination, and racial tension. A national strategy for increased home ownership must support private-public partnerships focused on the central cities and all lower-income families.

- Families receiving federal, state, and local housing subsidies should be able to use them either for buying or renting. For example, home ownership voucher programs could permit families to use vouchers for mortgage payments, utilities, or maintenance and repair.

- The distribution of federal low-income-housing and community-development subsidies should favor local partnerships that develop home ownership opportunities for low-income families.

- Federal and private sector programs to dispose of foreclosed properties in inner-city neighborhoods should

permit community organizations to acquire the properties. Such organizations could then allow low-income
families to invest "sweat equity" in the properties and
rehabilitate them. This could open the door to home
ownership for many such families.

• Laws governing mortgage foreclosures and reposses-
sions should ensure that repossessed properties are
quickly sold to new owners. In some states, the law
mandates long waiting periods between foreclosure
and resale: the result is vacant, deteriorating properties
and the prospect of wider urban wastelands.

There are many nonprofit enterprises, at the local and national
levels, that do marvelous work in local communities to increase
home ownership. The Enterprise Foundation has an explicit commitment to the goal that "all low-income people in the United
States should have the opportunity for fit and affordable housing
within a generation, and to move out of poverty into the main-
stream of American life."[64] The foundation has raised over $1 bil-
lion in equity grants and loans to finance over forty-two thousand
units of affordable housing. The Local Initiative Support Corporation (LISC) helps rebuild distressed neighborhoods by developing affordable housing and investing in job-creating enterprises. Its
National Equity Fund leverages corporate investment in affordable
homes with the federal tax credit available to people who invest
in low-income housing. Each year the Fannie Mae Foundation rec-
ognizes outstanding local nonprofits that are making it possible for
low-income families to obtain affordable housing. The award win-
ners are a source of innovation and ideas to be replicated around
the nation. One project that stands out is the Kentucky Mountain
Housing Development Corporation, which built new homes and
provided subsidized, low interest rate loans—as low as 1 percent—
to very low-income families and individuals. Many of the recipients

were homeless, developmentally or physically disabled, senior citizens, or single-parent families. Some went straight from hopelessness to home ownership.

10. Reduce the Cost of Housing

The single most effective way to bring home ownership within reach for first-time home buyers is to reduce the cost of the home they buy. In 1990, a 10 percent reduction in housing costs would have increased the number of households with the qualifying income to buy a home by 10 percent. A 20 percent reduction would have raised the number of qualifying households by 23 percent. The benefits of any such change would accrue disproportionately to minority households. If home prices for first-time buyers were to decline by 20 percent over the next ten years, the number of Hispanic households with enough income to qualify for home ownership would increase by 42 percent; the number of eligible African-American households would increase by 35 percent.[65]

Clearly this is a potent policy option. In practice, it would call for the preservation of existing affordable housing stock, the construction of a greater number of less expensive "starter homes," and a reduction in the land, capital, and construction costs of housing.

In 1991 the bipartisan Advisory Commission on Regulatory Barriers to Affordable Housing, led by former New Jersey governor Tom Kean and former Ohio congressman Thomas "Lud" Ashley, issued a report on the regulatory barriers that block the construction of more affordable housing. Their report, titled *Not in My Back Yard*, detailed the complex web of growth-control ordinances, exclusionary zoning, impact fees, subdivision rules, high property taxes, rent controls, building codes, and other regulations that drive up the cost of housing construction.[66] The elimination or reduction of such regulatory barriers would significantly increase the affordability of homes. The real-life examples uncovered by the commission are fascinating. In Bridgehampton, Long Island, a 102-acre residential construction project was halted when New York State environmental officials happened to find a tiger salamander, an endangered species, in a pond on the property. The project was stalled for more than a year, until the builder agreed not to build any homes within one hundred feet of the pond. To compensate for the delay and compliance costs, the builder then made a 50 percent cut in the number of homes that would be affordable for low- and moderate-income families.

In 1993, the National Association of Home Builders also studied the impact of regulations on home prices. The study examined three kinds of regulatory costs—land costs, impact fees and permits, and construction costs. These costs pushed home prices up by as much as 15 percent—and that didn't even account for the expenses associated with environmental compliance, wetlands and endangered species protection, and zoning requirements.[67] A national strategy for increased home ownership must increase the supply of new, inexpensive "starter" homes for first-time buyers.

- Localities and states, in concert with builders and community groups, should streamline housing construction by eliminating locally imposed barriers.

- The federal government should reform its own regulatory structure and ensure that environmental protection laws are enforced efficiently and in ways that are proportionate to the worth of the ends achieved.

- States, localities, the federal government, and the private sector should develop model building codes, ordinances, and standards, and they should be applied on a standardized basis across the nation.

Some states have cut through regulatory barriers to affordable housing. In 1969, Massachusetts passed an "anti–snob zoning law" that helped builders in the state's affordable housing construction program obtain building permits from local governments. As a result of that law and others that followed, the state can override local permit refusals when there is evidence that less than 10 percent of the jurisdiction's housing is affordable. The state can also withhold grant money from communities found to be "unreasonably restrictive of housing growth."[68] New Jersey is another state that has been breaking down barriers to affordable housing. A lawsuit filed in the 1970s by civil rights organizations argued that local zoning requirements and the denial of building permits for affordable housing constituted illegal discrimination. The New Jersey Supreme Court ruled that every developing community in New Jersey had a "constitutional obligation to contribute its fair share toward meeting its region's low- and moderate-income housing need."[69]

Costs can also be reduced by spreading them over a broader base. Today, funds for new community infrastructure come from the sale of new houses. In other words, the cost to the community of so-called entitlements—water, sewer, fire protection—for fifty new houses (or one hundred, or five hundred) are added to the price of those houses. So rather than having the broad community pay the costs of new growth, through taxes, more and more expense is piled on the people who are struggling to achieve home ownership. In many respects, this is the opposite of what happened in the past. Home builders point out that forty-five years ago, 69 percent of the cost of building a home was due to labor and building materials. Today that figure is 53 percent.[70] We have more and more people being priced out of home ownership because we are not spreading, over the broad community, the cost of expanding home ownership. Those who have already climbed the ladder are, in effect, pulling it up and leaving new arrivals stranded at the bottom.

If this continues, if for this reason and others we fall short of our home ownership potential, the consequences will be financially debilitating and socially disruptive. We will see a constantly rising demand for rental housing, along with less and less capacity to build it. The result will be a gradual increase in the percentage of lower-middle-class incomes devoted to housing. Housing costs will take a bigger and bigger chunk out of what people have to live on, which means that they will have less money to spend on education, nutrition, health care, and other necessities.

Today, the generally accepted rule of thumb is that if you spend about 30 percent of your income on shelter, that's all right, if not ideal. But millions of Americans, poor people and low- and middle-income families, spend up to 50 percent of their earnings on shelter. If more and more people lose the capacity to buy, if the cost of housing is further inflated by regulatory factors, if we have a bottle-neck in constructing new rental housing because of political and cost restraints, Americans will experience or witness even greater crowding.

Crowding is already the first thing that happens in a recession. More people live in a smaller space; so rather than a son or daughter finding an apartment of his or her own, they live indefinitely with Mom and/or Dad. Grandparents move in. We start having more densely populated places. Then what happens is the percentage of people's income spent on shelter soars. Today, the most common rental unit in America is the single-family home. It's not a high-rise apartment in New York City, or even a garden apartment out in Rockville, Maryland. It is a single-family house. If we don't facilitate home buying, there will be a bidding-up process in rents, as fewer and fewer people prove willing to buy. We will have more people spending more to live in less space. We will spend a lower percentage of national income on education and long-term investment. The United States will become economically weaker, socially tenser, and politically more divided.

Home Ownership at a Crossroads

I offer this strategy to expand home ownership at a time when the federal government's role in promoting housing is changing dramatically. Federal spending on housing programs is being drastically reduced. It's clear that the push to reorganize the federal role in housing is fundamental and bipartisan. Affordable housing programs simply don't have the standing in the federal budget that they had some years ago. Job training, welfare, health—federal programs that have defined how people relate to the government for more than a generation—are changing as well. The watchwords are devolution and local control.

The success of the strategy outlined above depends on the core strengths of our nation's housing system. These strengths must be preserved, even in the face of massive changes in the size and scope of the national commitment to housing. I include among these core strengths federal programs such as the low-income housing tax credit, which attracts investment in affordable rental housing for low-income families who are not yet ready to buy homes, and the FHA's loan guarantees, which help low- and moderate-income families and first-time home buyers achieve home ownership. Federal antidiscrimination laws such as the Fair Housing Act, the Community Reinvestment Act, and the Home Mortgage Disclosure Act are also core strengths of our nation's housing system, and we must preserve them and make them even more effective. We have to preserve and improve the ability of the secondary mortgage market to provide housing financing to low-, moderate-, and middle-income home buyers. And we must fight every effort to impose new home ownership taxes on home buyers or to eliminate the mortgage interest deduction, which makes it possible for so many working families to own homes of their own. These are among the many dimensions of the American system that put a priority and a value on housing. I believe that in the midst of changing federal priorities, we have to fight to preserve every policy and program that helps American families achieve home ownership.

While we must be committed to preserving the core strengths of our housing system, we must also take a very critical look at every dimension of the regulatory environment to make sure we don't end up with the worst of both worlds—less money but more regulation. In every city I visit, mayors tell me about their frustrations in dealing with a tangled web of complex federal regulations that stifle local creativity and innovation. In an era of diminishing resources for housing, we must be oriented toward local participation and control, so communities can be free to address their own priorities in the most productive way possible.

An orientation toward eliminating unneeded "strings" on the federal spending programs that remain must extend to those regulations and policies that drive up the cost of housing. I examined the need to reduce regulatory barriers to housing construction in the final segment of my strategy. Reducing the regulatory barriers that contribute so much to the rising cost of housing is more important than ever in an era of shrinking federal resources. Permits, building codes that are sometimes inappropriate, impact fees, exclusionary zoning, and policies for abandoned properties push the cost of building new housing and rehabilitating existing housing much higher than they need to be. If we can get these costs down, we can make substantial progress in housing affordability.

But as we devolve authority for housing programs to state and local governments, we have to make sure we don't forget the most important lesson we have learned in the affordable housing arena in the last twenty years: low- and moderate-income housing programs work best when combined with the right kind of social services, including child care and job training.

The need for a integrated approach to the needs of low- and moderate-income families who need shelter as well as social services is particularly important in the inner cities, where the most important single source of strength is the people and businesses who call it home. The wages, commitment, community dedication, and willingness to pursue innovative financing opportunities of these people and businesses are what will make the difference in cities over the long run. This doesn't mean cities should give up on trying to attract more investment from the outside, but as I go across the country and talk to mayors about what's going on in their cities, it's clear that their first priority is to maintain the tax base and keep people and businesses in the city. The successful cities of the future will be those that focus less on the "big dream" that resources will come in from the outside—whether from the federal government or from some other source—and instead focus on the comparative advantages possessed by the city and its citizens.

Finally, as federal resources for housing programs decline, we must redouble our efforts to create affordable rental housing for low-income families who aren't able to afford home ownership. As incomes have stagnated, fewer families are able to afford to buy homes. What that means is we're not going to be able to solve all the housing needs of our nation with home ownership. We will have to focus on more innovative ways to finance affordable rental housing, especially by rehabilitating the existing stock of housing in urban and rural communities.

Conclusion

Defining the Future of
the Housing Finance Industry

In a sense I suppose that I was destined, after years in public service and the investment sector, to find myself in the housing business. It's probably in my genes. After World War II, in 1946, my father and his partner, Myron Johnson, decided that they would go into the real estate business. They formed Johnson and Johnson Real Estate in 1946. At that time my dad was already forty-eight years old. He believed that with the returning veterans, homes would be built and children born—and the boom would come, if slowly, to Benson, Minnesota. In addition to real estate sales through Johnson and Johnson, he and his partner started building houses, one or two at a time.

His sister's husband, Ole Anfinson, dug basements. He had a basement-digging machine and a concrete-block assembly line, where he employed one or two people that actually made concrete blocks. My mother's brother, Al Rasmussen, was the manager of the Standard Lumber Yard, the source of the enterprise's building materials. Three of my father's brothers—Rudolph, Henry, and Bert— owned and operated Olsen Hardware, which was its source of tools, cabinets, and fasteners.

For many years, from 1946 until my father became ill with Parkinson's disease and had to slow down and retire in the early 1960s, real estate was his profession. He also was one of the incorporators of the Swift County Savings and Loan Association in 1951.

So he was involved in all aspects of housing. He was in home construction, sales, and home financing.

He was oriented toward government finance programs. He believed strongly that the federal government was making an essential contribution through the Federal Housing Administration—the FHA. I can recall how the first question he would ask when someone came into his office was whether or not he was a veteran, because if he was, that meant my father could secure financing for him through the Veterans Administration.

Johnson and Johnson had its office basically just off the lobby of the only hotel in town. When people came to Benson to look for a home, they would stay at the Paris Hotel, where they would see the Johnson and Johnson real estate sign. There were two desks in the office, my father's desk and his partner's. They did all the paperwork and filing themselves. The bank was three doors down. My dad would drive prospective home buyers around town, take them back to the office once they found a house, and then walk them over to the bank.

The Fannie Mae offices are bigger, the systems more complex, the customer base nationwide, but basically I'm in the same business as my father, and I only hope I do my job as well as he did his.

The 1990s bring new challenges. There are economic, structural, technological, demographic, and social forces at work in our nation today that my father never even imagined. A heightened awareness of racial discrimination in lending; the growth of the American population, fueled by immigration; advancements in affordability; an improved ability to manage the risk of lower down payment lending; the advances of technology and the maturity of the secondary market, providing a firm foundation for growth, stability, and liquidity in housing finance—all of these factors now converge to make the 1990s an optimal time for more Americans than ever before to fulfill their ambition to own a home. This can be a time of growth in home ownership unequaled in the postwar era.

My ultimate vision is of a housing, finance, and real estate system that is sufficiently flexible to tailor its products to fit the capa-
bility of every individual family. We should design a system that
shows people what they are able to afford and builds their momentum toward ownership by giving them savings vehicles, counseling,
information, and market understanding.

The possibilities are endless. If people have equity in their home
and want to use it, the system should make judgments about how
much to let them use depending on their age. If they are elderly,
house rich, and cash poor, the system should let them bring the cash
out. As the system becomes increasingly sophisticated, it can and
should function, in effect, as a financial adviser on housing economics for every family.

The system can and should allow for flexibility based on the economic capacity of each family. It should invite all families to think
about home ownership and to prepare for it. If they're renting, are
they renting in the most efficient way possible? If they're accumulating a down payment, are they accumulating it in the most efficient way possible? Are they managing their overall credit capacity
correctly? How can they do better in any of these areas?

At the outset, I wrote of what America will be like if a strategy
for increased home ownership is implemented. There will be millions of additional home owners, responding to a mortgage lending
industry that actively seeks their business and offers mortgage
financing options to meet their unique needs. Potential home owners will have incentives to save and to participate in counseling.
The housing finance industry will be what it could be—a model of
diversity, aggressively serving the growing portion of the population
made up of minorities and new immigrants, so that minorities will
own homes at the same rate as similarly situated whites. The housing construction industry will be freed from needless, duplicative
regulatory shackles, building more houses that are affordable for
first-time buyers. Distressed inner-city neighborhoods will be

strengthened as the civic and financial benefits of home ownership lead to less crime, better schools, improved infrastructures, and accumulated wealth.

I believe that the strategy proposed here should define the housing finance industry as we move into the next millennium. An America in which the home ownership rate moves steadily closer to the point where every person who wants to own a home does own a home is a goal worthy of our nation's proud history.

Notes

Introduction

1. As of the fourth quarter of 1995. U.S. Bureau of the Census. *Census Bureau Reports on Residential Vacancies and Homeownership.* (Press release.) February 1, 1996, p. 4, table 4.

2. Locke, J. *Two Treatises of Government.* (P. Laslett, ed.). Cambridge, England: Cambridge University Press, 1988, p. 350.

3. Fannie Mae. *Fannie Mae National Housing Survey, 1994.* Washington, D.C.: Fannie Mae, 1994, p. 7. The 88 percent figure was derived by adding a figure representing 67 percent of current renters to the number of current homeowners. (The 67 percent figure reflects those who would like to own but rent due to financial circumstances.) In 1993 there were approximately 34 million rented households and 63 million owner-occupied households.

4. Eggers, F. J., and Burke, P. E. "Simulating the Impact on Homeownership Rates of Strategies to Increase Ownership by Low-Income and Minority Households." Paper presented at the 1995 Fannie Mae Annual Housing Conference, Washington, D.C., May 24, 1995.

5. Joint Center for Housing Studies. *The State of the Nation's Housing, 1994.* Cambridge, Mass.: Joint Center for Housing Studies, Harvard University, 1994, p. 11.

Chapter One

1. Beyer, G. *Housing and Society.* New York: Macmillan, 1965, p. 249.

2. From President Clinton's address to the National Association of Home Builders, January 30, 1995.

3. Rosow, I. "Home Ownership Motives." *American Sociological Review,* 1948, *13,* 751.

4. Muller, H. M. *Urban Home Ownership: A Socioeconomic Analysis with Emphasis on Philadelphia.* (Ph.D. dissertation.) Philadelphia, 1947.

5. Hart-Teeter Research. *Housing Monitor, 1993: A Survey of American Opinion on Housing Issues.* Washington, D.C.: Hart-Teeter Research, 1993.

6. Delany, S., and Delany, A. E., with Hearth, A. H. *Having Our Say: The Delany Sisters' First 100 Years.* New York: Kodansha International, 1993, pp. 193–194.

7. Lueck, T. J. "Buying a Home Is Still an American Goal." *New York Times,* June 30, 1991, sec. 10, p. 1.

8. Hart-Teeter Research, *Housing Monitor, 1993,* table 42.

9. Green, R. K., and White, M. J. *Measuring the Benefits of Homeowning: Effects on Children.* (Working Paper No. 93.) Chicago: Center for the Study of the Economy and the State, University of Chicago, 1994, p. 1.

10. Gans, H. J. *The Levittowners.* New York: Columbia University Press, 1982.

11. Gans, *Levittowners,* pp. 297–298, note 27.

12. Hart-Teeter Research, *Housing Monitor, 1993,* table 39.

13. Jackson, K. T. *Crabgrass Frontier: The Suburbanization of the United States.* New York: Oxford University Press, 1985, p. 50.

14. Dean, J. P. *Home Ownership: Is It Sound?* New York: HarperCollins, 1945, p. 2.

15. Caplow, T. "Home Ownership and Location Preferences in a Minneapolis Sample." *American Sociological Review,* 1948, *13,* 725–726.

16. Caplow, "Home Ownership and Location Preferences," p. 728.

17. Caplow, "Home Ownership and Location Preferences," p. 730.

18. Caplow, "Home Ownership and Location Preferences," pp. 727–729, table 2.

19. Tobey, R., Wetherall, C., and Brigham, J. "Moving Out and Settling In: Residential Mobility, Home Owning, and the Public Enframing of Citizenship, 1921–1950." *American Historical Review*, 1990, 95, 1403, table 2.

20. Tobey, Wetherall, and Brigham, "Moving Out and Settling In," pp. 1406–1407.

21. Speare, A., Jr. "Home Ownership, Lifecycle Stage, and Resident Mobility." *Demography*, November 1970, pp. 449–458.

22. Gans, *Levittowners*, p. 298, note 34.

23. Kingston, P. W., Thompson, J.L.P., and Eichar, D. M. "The Politics of Homeownership." *American Politics Quarterly*, 1984, 12, 145, table 3.

24. Kingston, Thompson, and Eichar, "Politics of Homeownership," p. 146.

25. Estimates by Lawrence Q. Newton of Fannie Mae, using data in Kingston, Thompson, and Eichar, "Politics of Homeownership," 141, table 1, taking into account votes cast for John Anderson and other independent candidates and assuming that Anderson received votes from "independent Republicans" while other independent candidates received votes from "independents."

26. Kingston, Thompson, and Eichar, "Politics of Homeownership," p. 140.

27. Kingston, Thompson, and Eichar, "Politics of Homeownership," p. 141, table 1.

28. Kain, J. F., and Quigley, J. M. "Housing Market Discrimination, Home Ownership, and Savings Behavior." *American Economic Review*, 1972, 62, 263–277.

29. National Association of Home Builders. *Forecast of Housing Activity*, August 1992, pp. 7–8.

30. Engels, F. *The Housing Question*. New York: International Publishers, 1935 edition, p. 35.

31. Castells, M. "Advanced Capitalism, Collective Consumption and Urban Contradictions: New Sources of Inequality and New Models for Change." In R. Lindberg and R. Alford (eds.), *Stress and Contradiction in Modern Capitalism*. Lexington, Mass.: Heath, 1975, p. 183.

32. Smith, B. A., and Saderion, Z. "Home Owning in the 1990s." *Society*, September–October 1992, p. 36.

33. Smith, A. *Paper Money*. New York: Dell, 1981, p. 76.

34. Jackson, *Crabgrass Frontier*, p. 52.

35. Gans, *Levittowners*, p. viii.

36. U.S. Bureau of the Census. *American Housing Survey, 1993*. Washington, D.C.: U.S. Government Printing Office, 1993, pp. 54–55, table 2-9.

37. Duany, A., and Plater-Zyberk, E. "The Second Coming of the American Small Town." *Wilson Quarterly*, Winter 1992, 22.

38. Blum, T. C., and Kingston, P. W. "Homeownership and Social Attachment." *Social Perspectives*, April 1984, 175.

39. Peter D. Hart Research Associates. *National Housing Monitor*. Washington, D.C.: Peter D. Hart Research Associates, 1994, ques. 8. The *National Housing Monitor* contains the unpublished tabulations of survey data; the *Fannie Mae National Housing Survey* is the published report of survey findings.

40. Hart Research Associates, *National Housing Monitor*, ques. 8.

41. Fannie Mae, *National Housing Survey*, 1994, p. 25. Twenty-eight percent of renters who are "somewhat likely to buy" consider "not knowing how to get started" a major obstacle to buying a home, while only 22 percent would consider "finding the right neighborhood" an obstacle.

42. U.S. Bureau of the Census, *American Housing Survey, 1993*, pp. 54–55, table 2-9.

43. Fannie Mae, *National Housing Survey*, 1994, pp. 24–25.

44. Hart-Teeter Research. *Housing Monitor, 1992: A Survey of American Opinion on Housing Issues*. Washington, D.C.: Hart-Teeter Research, 1992, pp. 5–7.

45. U.S. Bureau of the Census, *American Housing Survey, 1993*, pp. 122–123, table 3-15.

46. Brinner, R. E., Lasky, M., and Wyss, D. *Residential Impacts of Flat Tax Legislation*. Lexington, Mass.: DRI/McGraw-Hill, 1995.

Chapter Two

1. Ely, J. W., Jr. *The Guardian of Every Other Right*. New York: Oxford University Press, 1992, p. 17.

2. Dietz, G. *The Federalist*. Baltimore: Johns Hopkins University Press, 1960, p. 82.

3. *Vanhorne's Lessee v. Dorrance*, 2 U.S. 304 (1795).

4. *Calder v. Bull*, 3 U.S. 386 (1798).

5. *Buchanan v. Warley*, 245 U.S. 60 (1917).

6. Katz, S. N. "Thomas Jefferson and the Right to Property in Revolutionary America." *Journal of Law and Economics*, 1976, *19*, 82.

7. Billington, R. A. *Westward Expansion: A History of the American Frontier*. (2nd ed.) New York: Macmillan, 1960, p. 58.

8. Fish, G. S. (ed.). *The Story of Housing*. New York: Macmillan, 1979, pp. 10–11.

9. Fish, *Story of Housing*, p. 27.

10. Billington, *Westward Expansion*, p. 84.

11. Neely, M. E., Jr. *The Last Best Hope of Earth: Abraham Lincoln and the Promise of America*. Cambridge, Mass.: Harvard University Press, 1993, pp. 3–6.

12. Fish, *Story of Housing*, pp. 55–56.

13. Billington, *Westward Expansion*, p. 700.

14. "The first income tax laws, though short-lived, are important in housing, since they served as models for the income tax laws of the 20th century. The provisions of the income tax laws of the 1860s of relevance to housing were the deductions permitted for payments of state and local taxes and for interest on personal indebtedness. These exclusions applied to taxes on real estate and interest on home mortgages as well as to other kinds of taxes and interest payments. . . . One reason for adopting an income tax to help finance the Civil war rather than a tax on real estate was that a tax on land would fall 'with very heavy, if not ruinous effect upon the great agricultural states of the West and Southwest.' One member of Congress stated: 'I cannot go home and tell my constituents that I voted for a bill that would allow a man, a millionaire, who has put his entire property into stock, to be exempt from taxation, while a farmer who lives by his side must pay a tax.'" From Margaret Woods, "Housing and Cities: 1790 to 1890," in Fish, *Story of Housing*, p. 108.

15. Billington, *Westward Expansion*, p. 672.

16. U.S. Bureau of National Affairs. *Excerpts from the Clinton FY 1995 Budget Submitted to Congress February 7, 1994*. (Special supplement.) February 8, 1994, p. S-241.

17. Fish, *Story of Housing*, p. 186.

18. Fish, *Story of Housing*, p. 178.

19. Tobey, Wetherall, and Brigham, "Moving Out and Settling In," p. 1416.

20. Tobey, Wetherall, and Brigham, "Moving Out and Settling In," p. 1417.

21. Fish, *Story of Housing*, p. 189.

22. Carey Winston provides an excellent analysis of the Home Owners' Loan Corporation in Fish, *Story of Housing*, pp. 188–194.

23. U.S. Senate. Committee on Government Operations. Subcommittee on Executive Reorganization. *The Federal Role in Urban Affairs*, 89th Cong., 2nd sess., December 30, 1966, pp. 41–42. "The [FHA] reform accomplished many extremely important purposes: 1) The volume of local housing credit was increased because of the Federal insurance, and savings banks and other conservative lending institutions increased their participation in residential financing; 2) The relative uniformity of the Federal guarantee, as distinct from the variety of security afforded by conventional mortgages in different states and localities, encouraged the flow of mortgage credit across state lines as insurance companies and other non-local lenders—primarily relying on the Federal insurance—made mortgage funds available, generally through mortgage banking firms and other loan correspondents in distant areas; 3) Many families with small savings, particularly younger families, were brought into the housing market because of the lower down payment made possible by the FHA insurance; 4) Families of moderate income were brought into the home-buying market, particularly as general economic conditions improved, by the lower monthly costs which resulted from lower interest rates and longer terms of repayment; 5) The risk of future foreclosures was greatly reduced because the level repayment plan, having first eased the burden of repayment in early, low-income years, provided for steady and complete amortization over

the life of the mortgage; 6) the FHA insurance provided a steadier flow of credit for rental housing; and 7) The increasing size of the housing market and the increasing flow of mortgage funds, both locally and across state lines, made larger-scale and more efficient housing construction possible."

24. Jones, J., and Angly, E. *Fifty Billion Dollars: My Thirteen Years with the RFC.* New York: Macmillan, 1951, pp. 148–149.

25. Day, K. *S&L Hell.* New York: Norton, 1993, p. 44. Day writes: "Thrifts acting alone could buy and sell only loans that originated in their communities and even there had no organized way to match buyers with sellers. In contrast, originators of FHA-backed loans could buy or sell them to lenders across the country via Fannie Mae."

Chapter Three

1. Whitman, S. *V Is for Victory: The American Home Front During World War II.* Minneapolis, Minn.: Lerner, 1993, pp. 35–36.

2. Teaford, J. C. *The Twentieth-Century American City.* Baltimore: Johns Hopkins University Press, 1986, p. 100.

3. "William J. Levitt, Pioneer of Postwar Suburbia, Dies." *Washington Post,* January 30, 1994, p. B6.

4. Teaford, *Twentieth-Century American City,* p. 101.

5. Keerdoja, E. "Mr. Levitt's Town." *Newsweek,* October 11, 1976, p. 18.

6. Bressler, M. "The Myers Case: An Instance of Successful Racial Invasion." *Social Problems,* 1960, 8, 126–142.

7. Kowinski, W. S. "Indoor Shopping Malls 30 Years Old." *New York Times,* October 9, 1986, p. 13.

8. Smith, *Paper Money,* p. 84.

9. Bureau of National Affairs, "Excerpts," p. S-241.

10. Ginnie Mae has permitted the originators of mortgages to "pool" VA and FHA loans, with Ginnie Mae insuring the mortgages for a fee. This allows investors to receive the monthly interest on mortgage payments without worrying about the borrower defaulting. Fannie Mae, on several occasions, particularly during the 1970s, has

worked with Ginnie Mae on "Tandem Plans" and other arrangements that provided subsidies and a secondary market for homes sold to low-income families. Ginnie Mae played an important role in making thirty-year mortgages an industry standard.

11. Smith, *Paper Money*, p. 79.

12. U.S. Bureau of the Census. *Historical Statistics of the United States, Colonial Times to 1970, Part 2.* (Series N170.) White Plains, N.Y.: Kraus International, 1989, p. 640; U.S. Bureau of the Census. *Statistical Abstract of the United States, 1982–83.* Washington, D.C.: U.S. Government Printing Office, 1983, p. 747, tables 1339, 1340.

13. Bureau of the Census, *American Housing Survey, 1993*, p. 38, table 2-1.

14. U.S. Bureau of the Census. *Statistical Abstract of the United States, 1994.* Washington, D.C.: U.S. Government Printing Office, 1994, p. 730, table 1202.

Chapter Four

1. U.S. Bureau of the Census. *Historical Statistics of the United States, Colonial Times to 1970, Part 1.* (Series A 288–319.) White Plains, N.Y.: Kraus International, 1989, p. 41; Bureau of the Census, *Statistical Abstract, 1994,* p. 58, table 66.

2. U.S. Bureau of the Census. *Statistical Abstract of the United States, 1995.* Washington, D.C.: U.S. Government Printing Office, 1995, p. 66, table 79.

3. Bureau of the Census, *American Housing Survey, 1993*, p. 54, table 2-9.

4. Joint Center for Housing Studies, *The State of the Nation's Housing, 1993.* Cambridge, Mass.: Joint Center for Housing Studies, Harvard University, 1993, p. 27, table A-5.

5. Joint Center for Housing Studies, *The State of the Nation's Housing, 1993,* p. 11, exhibit 14.

6. Joint Center for Housing Studies, *The State of the Nation's Housing, 1993,* p. 11.

7. U.S. Bureau of the Census. *Household Wealth and Asset Ownership, 1991.* Washington, D.C.: U.S. Government Printing Office, 1994, p. xiii, table H.

8. Bureau of the Census, *American Housing Survey*, 1981–1993.

9. Lea, M. J., and Bernstein, S. A. *International Housing Finance Sourcebook, 1995*. Chicago: International Union of Housing Finance Institutions, 1995.

10. Miles, D. "Housing and the Wider Economy in the Short and Long Run." *National Institute Economic Review*, February 1992, p. 76.

11. "UK Money-Go-Round: Five Years On, and Gloom Still Hangs over Housing." *Daily Telegraph*, September 3, 1994, p. 1.

12. Stowe, R. "The Great Housing Bust in Britain." *Mortgage Banking*, March 1993, p. 31.

13. Sanger, D. E. "Hosokawa's Report, à la Clinton." *New York Times*, February 12, 1994, p. 4.

Chapter Five

1. Joint Center for Housing Studies, *The State of the Nation's Housing, 1994*, p. 30.

2. Brown, J., and Bennington, C. *Racial Redlining! A Study of Racial Discrimination by Banks and Mortgage Companies in the United States*. Washington, D.C.: Essential Information, 1993, p. 6.

3. Interagency Task Force on Fair Lending. *Policy Statement*. Washington, D.C.: Department of Housing and Urban Development, March 1994, pp. 15–17.

4. Hart Research Associates, *National Housing Monitor*, ques. 36b.

5. Interagency Task Force, *Policy Statement*, p. 5.

6. Munnell, A. H., Browne, L. E., McEneaney, J., and Tootell, G.M.B. *Mortgage Lending in Boston: Interpreting HMDA Data*. (Federal Reserve Bank of Boston Working Paper No. 92–97.) Boston: Federal Reserve Bank of Boston, October 1992.

7. Munnell and others, *Mortgage Lending in Boston*, p. 2.

8. Munnell and others, *Mortgage Lending in Boston*, p. 10.

9. It should be noted that appraisers have been accused of presenting lower estimates of a property in affluent areas once they discover the current occupant is African American. This hurts the African-

his or her race, since lenders generally will loan no more than 80 or 90 percent of a home's appraised value.

10. Munnell and others, *Mortgage Lending in Boston*, p. 12.

11. Munnell and others, *Mortgage Lending in Boston*, pp. 2–3.

12. Carr, J. H., and Megbolugbe, I. F. *The Federal Reserve Bank of Boston Study on Mortgage Lending Revisited*. Fannie Mae Working Paper. Washington, D.C.: Federal National Mortgage Association, Office of Housing Research, 1993, p. v.

13. Dedman, W. "Atlanta Blacks Losing in Home Loans Scramble." *Atlanta Journal and Constitution*, May 1, 1988, p. 1.

14. Dedman, "Atlanta Blacks," p. 2.

15. "Rights Leaders Call for Action Against Banks." *Detroit Free Press*, July 26, 1988, p. 1A.

16. "Black Areas Get Fewer Home Loans: Banks Lend to White Areas In Detroit by 3–1 Margin." *Detroit Free Press*, July 24, 1988, p. 1A.

17. "Home Inequity." *Newsday*, August 14, 1994, p. A7.

18. "U.S., Chevy Chase FSB Discussing Bias Probe: Talks on Branch Sites to Involve New View of Law." *Washington Post*, August 20, 1994, p. F1; "Chevy Chase Settles Case over Bias." *Washington Post*, August 23, 1994, p. A1.

19. Turner, M. A., Struyk, R. J., and Yinger, J. *Housing Discrimination Study*. Washington, D.C.: Urban Institute and Syracuse University, 1991.

20. Feagin, J. R., and Sikes, M. P. *Living with Racism: The Black Middle-Class Experience*. Boston: Beacon Press, 1994.

21. Feagin and Sikes, *Living with Racism*, p. 238.

22. Feagin and Sikes, pp. 238–239.

23. Feagin and Sikes, pp. 241–242.

24. Feagin and Sikes, pp. 239–240.

25. Minerbrook, S. "Homeownership Anchors the Middle Class: But Lending Games Sink Many Prospective Owners." *Emerge*, September 1993, p. 42.

26. National Advisory Commission on Civil Disorders. *Report of the*

National Advisory Commission on Civil Disorders. New York: Dutton, 1968, p. 1.

27. Orfield, G. "Separate Societies: Have the Kerner Warnings Come True?" in F. R. Harris and R. W. Wilkins (eds.), *Quiet Riots.* New York: Pantheon Books, 1988, p. 108.

28. Seligman, D. "Keeping Up." *Fortune,* August 22, 1994, p. 213.

29. Joint Center for Housing Studies, *The State of the Nation's Housing, 1994,* p. 30, table A-7.

30. Swift, M. "Appeal of City Life is Fading for Middle-Class Hispanics." *Hartford Courant,* January 30, 1994, p. A1. The article points out that the number of Hispanics who moved to the suburbs during the 1980s surpasses the population of Connecticut by three hundred thousand.

31. "In Marketing, Exit Black Enterprise." *Wall Street Journal,* July 20, 1994, p. B1; De Witt, K. "Suburban Expansion Fed by an Influx of Minorities." *New York Times,* August 15, 1994, p. A1

32. Close, E. *The Rage of a Privileged Class.* New York: HarperCollins, 1993, p. 191.

Chapter Six

1. Estimate by Lawrence Q. Newton of Fannie Mae, from data on the number of single-family home mortgage loans that the Federal Housing Administration, the Farmer's Home Administration, and the Department of Veterans Affairs have insured, guaranteed, or made from the beginning of their respective programs to the end of September 1994.

2. Hughes, J. W. "Clashing Demographics: Homeownership and Affordability Dilemmas." *Housing Policy Debate,* 1991, *2,* 1218.

3. Minority population and household projections by Lawrence Q. Newton of Fannie Mae.

4. U.S. census figures for 1980 and 1990.

5. Day, J. C. "Population Projections of the United States, by Age, Sex, Race, and Hispanic Origin, 1993 to 2050." (U.S. Bureau of the Census Current Population Report No. P25–1104.) Washington, D.C.: U.S. Government Printing Office, 1993.

6. Joint Center for Housing Studies, *The State of the Nation's Housing, 1994*, p. 28, table A-5.

7. Johnston, W. B., Packer, A. E., and U.S. Department of Labor. *Workforce 2000: Work and Workers for the 21st Century*. Indianapolis: Hudson Institute, 1987.

8. Fullerton, H. N. "Labor Force Projections: The Baby Boom Moves On." *Monthly Labor Review*, November 1991, p. 41, table 5.

9. Day, "Population Projections," p. xvi, table F.

10. Day, "Population Projections," p. 26, table 2; U.S. census figures for 1960 and 1990.

11. Gyourko, J., and Linneman, P. "Affordability of the American Dream: An Examination of the Last 30 Years." *Journal of Housing Research*, 1993, *4*, 39–72.

12. National Association of Realtors. *Home Sales Yearbook, 1990*. Washington, D.C.: National Association of Realtors, 1991, p. 37, table 22; *Real Estate Outlook*, November 1995, p. 14.

13. Gyourko and Linneman, "Affordability of the American Dream," p. 48.

14. Gyourko and Linneman, p. 49.

15. Fannie Mae, *National Housing Survey,1994*, pp. 26–27.

16. Fannie Mae's outreach, consumer advertising, and home buyer education activities were launched by the corporation; on April 1, 1996, responsibility for these activities was transferred to the Fannie Mae Foundation. James A. Johnson is chairman of both Fannie Mae and the Fannie Mae Foundation.

17. Joint Center for Housing Studies, *The State of the Nation's Housing, 1994*, p. 27, table A-4; tabulations from U.S. Bureau of the Census, *American Housing Survey*, 1973, 1976, and 1980; and Bureau of the Census. *Current Population Survey*. Washington, D.C.: U.S. Government Printing Office, 1983, 1987, 1989, and 1992.

18. Downs, A. "Policy Directions Concerning Racial Discrimination in U.S. Housing Markets." *Housing Policy Debate*, 1992, *3*, 687.

19. Wienk, R. "Discrimination in Urban Credit Markets: What We Don't Know and Why We Don't Know It." *Housing Policy Debate*, 1992, 3, 237.

20. Federal Reserve Bank of Cleveland, Fourth District. *Community Reinvestment Forum*. (Special issue.) Cleveland, Ohio: Federal Reserve Bank of Cleveland, 1994, p. 7.

21. Lindsay, L. B. "How to Lend a Hand." *Wall Street Journal*, November 2, 1994, p. A14.

22. Bradbury, K. L., Case, K. E., and Dunham, C. R. *Geographic Patterns of Mortgage Lending in Boston, 1982–1987*. Boston: Federal Reserve Bank of Boston, 1989.

23. Interagency Task Force, *Policy Statement*.

24. U.S. Bureau of the Census. *Geographical Mobility: March 1990 to March 1991*. (Current Population Report No. P20–463.) Washington, D.C.: U.S. Government Printing Office, 1992.

25. U.S. Department of Commerce and U.S. Department of Housing and Urban Development. *American Housing Survey for the United States in 1991*. Washington, D.C.: U.S. Government Printing Office, 1991.

26. Federal National Mortgage Association (Fannie Mae). *Anecdotes: "Showing America a New Way Home."* Washington, D.C.: Federal National Mortgage Association, 1994, p. 17.

27. Mersenheimer, J. R., Jr. "How Do Immigrants Fare in the U.S. Labor Market?" *Monthly Labor Review*, December 1992, p. 16, table 11, and p. 17.

28. Joint Center for Housing Studies, *The State of the Nation's Housing, 1994*, p. 30, table A-7; tabulations of U.S. census figures for 1980 and 1990 by Brad German of the National Association of Home Builders.

29. Rose, F. "The Outlook: Latest Immigrants Face Tough Job Problems." *Wall Street Journal*, November 28, 1994, p. A1.

30. United Neighborhood Organization of Chicago (UNO). *Naturalization Potential in 1995 and Beyond*. Chicago: United Neighborhood Organization of Chicago, 1994.

31. Black, C. "Chao from Dot. Ave." *Boston Globe Sunday Magazine*, September 12, 1993, p. 36.

32. Black, "Chao," p. 45.

33. Black, "Chao," p. 46.

34. Chung, L. S. "Oakland's Chinatown Charging Ahead: Shops, Residents Bring New Life to Downtown." *San Francisco Chronicle*, November 30, 1992, p. A15.

35. Voboril, M. "Port of Entry: Immigrants Thrive in New York's 'Informal Economy.'" *Newsday*, June 21, 1993, p. 31.

36. Rosenblatt, R. "Sunset, Sunrise: Brooklyn's Immigrant Renewal." *New Republic*, December 27, 1993, p. 21.

37. Rosenblatt, "Sunset, Sunrise," p. 23.

38. Fix, M., and Passel, J. *Immigration and Immigrants: Setting the Record Straight*. Washington, D.C.: Urban Institute, 1994.

39. UNO, *Naturalization Potential*, p. 1.

40. UNO, *Naturalization Potential*, p. 1.

41. Fannie Mae, *Anecdotes*, p. 25.

42. Fannie Mae, *Anecdotes*, p. 24.

43. Fannie Mae, *National Housing Survey, 1994*, pp. 24–25; Mortgage Bankers Association of America and the Gallup Organization. *Study on Barriers to Homeownership and Perceptions of Discrimination in Mortgage Lending*. (Executive summary.) Washington, D.C.: Mortgage Bankers Association of America, 1994, p. 8.

44. Joint Center for Housing Studies, *The State of the Nation's Housing, 1994*, p. 11.

45. Haurin, D. R., Wachter, S. M., and Hendershott, P. "Wealth Accumulation and Housing Choices of Young Households: An Exploratory Investigation." Paper presented at the Fannie Mae Roundtable on Understanding Household Savings for Homeownership, Washington D.C., November 9, 1994.

46. Haurin, Wachter, and Hendershott, "Wealth Accumulation."

47. Mayer, C. J., and Englehardt, G. V. "Gifts, Down Payments, and Housing Affordability." Paper presented at the Fannie Mae Roundtable on Understanding Household Savings for Homeownership, Washington, D.C., November 9, 1994.

48. Spain, D. "New Households, Old Story: Homeownership for Female Householders Since 1950." Paper presented at the Fannie Mae Roundtable on Understanding Household Savings for Homeownership, Washington, D.C., November 9, 1994.

49. Lea, M. J., and Renaud, B. "Contract Savings for Housing." Paper presented at the Fannie Mae Roundtable on Understanding Household Savings for Homeownership, Washington, D.C., November 9, 1994.

50. Linneman, P. D., and Wachter, S. B. "The Impacts of Borrowing Constraints on Home Ownership." *AREUEA Journal*, 17, 389–402.

51. Fannie Mae, *Anecdotes*, p. 12.

52. Willis-Boyland, A. *Housing Opportunities: Building on Tradition.* Washington, D.C.: Savings and Community Bankers of America, 1993, pp. 12–13.

53. National Association of Home Builders. *Economic Stimulus, Job Creation, and Housing.* Paper presented to the presidential transition office, November 25, 1992.

54. Federal National Mortgage Association. *Report of Fannie Mae on Underwriting Guidelines to the Secretary of Housing and Urban Development, the House Committee on Banking, Finance and Urban Affairs, and the Senate Committee on Banking, Housing and Urban Affairs, Pursuant to P.L. 102–550, Section 1354.* Washington, D.C.: Federal National Mortgage Association, October 28, 1993, p. 42.

55. Estimates by Lawrence Q. Newton of Fannie Mae, using data from the U.S. Bureau of the Census (single-family housing starts and percentage of new homes sold in cash), National Association of Realtors (existing home sales and percentage of existing homes sold in cash), Department of Housing and Urban Development (FHA-insured mortgages), and the Federal Housing Finance Board (distribution of loans by loan-to-value ratios).

56. Fannie Mae, *Anecdotes*, p. 3.

57. Fannie Mae, *Anecdotes*, p. 27.

58. U.S. Department of Energy. *Household Energy Consumption and Expenditures, 1990*. Washington, D.C.: U.S. Government Printing Office, February 1993, p. 60, table 18.

59. Prindle, W. R., and Reid, M. W. *Energy Efficiency: A Key to Affordable Housing*. Washington, D.C.: Alliance to Save Energy, January 28, 1988, p. 10, table 6.

60. Fannie Mae, *Anecdotes*, p. 9.

61. Downs, A. *New Visions for Metropolitan America*. Washington, D.C.: Brookings Institution, 1994, p. 70.

62. Downs, *New Visions*, p. 79.

63. Bradbury, K., Downs A., and Small, K. A. *Urban Decline and the Future of American Cities*. Washington, D.C.: Brookings Institution, 1982, p. 12.

64. Enterprise Foundation press release, October 1994.

65. Fannie Mae projections by Lawrence Q. Newton.

66. U.S. Advisory Commission on Regulatory Barriers to Affordable Housing. *Not in My Back Yard: Removing Barriers to Affordable Housing*. Washington, D.C.: U.S. Department of Housing and Urban Development, 1991.

67. German, B. "Under Siege: What Regulations Cost Builders and Buyers." *Builder*, August 1993, pp. 46–51.

68. U.S. Advisory Commission, *Not in My Back Yard*, p. 7-4.

69. U.S. Advisory Commission, *Not in My Back Yard*, p. 7-4.

70. National Association of Home Builders. *Housing Backgrounder*, April 1992, p. 33.

The Author

Few individuals in America today can lay claim to advancing the goal of home ownership more than James A. Johnson. As chairman and CEO of Fannie Mae, Johnson has dedicated the nation's largest financial institution to reducing housing costs, eliminating mortgage discrimination, and expanding opportunities for the millions of Americans who dream of owning their own home.

During Johnson's five years at the head of Fannie Mae, the company has done more than $1 trillion of business, financed homes for more than 12 million families, earned more than $9 billion, increased its market value by nearly $27 billion, and grown to be the nation's largest company in terms of assets, surpassing American Express, Citicorp, General Motors, Ford, and General Electric. He has restructured Fannie Mae and formed new partnerships with hundreds of public and private sector organizations with one thing in mind: getting the money for home loans into the hands of the millions of Americans who have been shut off from access to affordable mortgage credit in the past.

Johnson came to Fannie Mae via academia, politics, public policy, and Wall Street. He was a faculty member at Princeton and served in the United States Senate. In addition he was managing director in corporate finance at Lehman Brothers, Vice President Walter Mondale's executive assistant and chair of his presidential campaign in 1984, and president of the Washington consulting firm

Public Strategies. Johnson is also chairman of the board of trustees of the John F. Kennedy Center for the Performing Arts, chairman of the board of trustees of the Brookings Institution, and a director of a number of major corporations and charitable institutions, including the Carnegie Corporation of New York, the Dayton Hudson Corporation, Kaufman and Broad Home Corporation, and United Health Care Corporation.

Index